Anonymous

Pictures of travel in far-off lands

A companion to the study of geography of Central America

Anonymous

Pictures of travel in far-off lands
A companion to the study of geography of Central America

ISBN/EAN: 9783337205027

Printed in Europe, USA, Canada, Australia, Japan

Cover: Foto ©Andreas Hilbeck / pixelio.de

More available books at **www.hansebooks.com**

GAUCHO. Page 82.

PICTURES OF TRAVEL

IN

FAR-OFF LANDS:

A Companion to the Study of Geography.

SOUTH AMERICA.

"Home-keeping youths have ever homely wits;
....I would entreat your company
To see the wonders of the world abroad."
SHAKSPEARE.

LONDON:
T. NELSON AND SONS, PATERNOSTER ROW;
EDINBURGH; AND NEW YORK.

1871.

Preface.

This volume is the first of a Series designed to render the study of Geography attractive to the young. Our plan is to present a bright and vivid picture to the imagination, instead of dry details of facts to the memory, which, when learned as a task, are too often forgotten. We have endeavoured to connect with the description of each country some interesting narrative or adventure taken from works of Travel, Biography, and History, that may tend to impress upon the reader's mind some of the characteristic features of the land in which they took place.

Contents.

FIRST DIVISION.
SOUTHERN COUNTRIES OF SOUTH AMERICA.

TERRA DEL FUEGO.	STATES OF LA PLATA,
PATAGONIA.	URUGUAY, BUENOS
CHILI AND ITS ISLANDS.	AYRES, PARAGUAY.

CHAPTER I.
TERRA DEL FUEGO.

General Description of the New World. Terra del Fuego—Cape Horn — Climate — Plants and Animals — People — Story of the Martyrs of Fuegia, ... 13

CHAPTER II.
PATAGONIA.

Extent—Climate—Animals—People—Savage Life—Mode of Hunting—Marriage among the Patagonians—Adventures of Mr. Bousne, or "Life among the Giants," 34

CHAPTER III.
CHILI AND ITS ISLANDS.

Description of Chili—Its Mines—Animals—People—Conquest by the Spaniards — The Islands of Chili, Juan Fernandez — Adventures of Alexander Selkirk, the real "Robinson Crusoe," 53

CHAPTER IV.
THE PAMPAS.

General Description—Storms in the Pampas—People—The Gauchos, or Indians of the Pampas — Other Indian Tribes — Terrible Adventure in the Pampas, ... 78

CHAPTER V.
STATE OF LA PLATA, ETC.

La Plata—Republic of Paraguay—Uruguay—Buenos Ayres—Story of Maldonata, ... 99

SECOND DIVISION.
CENTRAL COUNTRIES.

BRAZIL.   BOLIVIA.   PERU.

CHAPTER VI.
THE EMPIRE OF BRAZIL.

General Description—Its vast Rivers—First Discovery and Subsequent History—**Arrival of** Don John VI. from Portugal—Brazil **Declared a** Kingdom—Don John Returns to Portugal—Revolution — **Brazil** Acknowledged Independent — Don Pedro I. **Crowned** Emperor—His Abdication—The Present Emperor Don Pedro II. 105

CHAPTER VII.
RIO DE JANEIRO.

First Discovery of the Bay—Origin of the Name—**The Beauty of the** Scenery—The Sugar-Loaf—The **Organ** Mountains—Commercial Importance of Rio de Janeiro — **Its** Fine Harbour — **General** Aspect of the City, ... 110

CHAPTER VIII.
VEGETABLE PRODUCTIONS OF BRAZIL.

Extent of Brazil—Its Vast Resources—Its Productions, **Mineral** and Vegetable—The Manioc Root— Its Use by **the Natives** — By the Portuguese — Modes of Preparing it — Drink made from it — The Palm **Tree — Its Uses** — **The** Caoutchouc, or Gum-Elastic Tree—The Milk Tree, &c. 120

CHAPTER IX.
THE ANIMALS OF BRAZIL.

A River Voyage—Birds and Monkeys—Food of the Natives—Salutation in Brazil—The Jaguar—Its Habits—A Story from Catlin's

CONTENTS.

Travels — The Feast Interrupted — The Disturber Killed — The Tapir — The Ant-eater — The Iguana — Birds and Insects, ... **139**

CHAPTER X.
MINAS-GERAES—ITS DIAMONDS AND ITS COFFEE.

Extent of the Province — Its Fertility — Its Minerals — Precious Stones — Diamonds — The Star of the South — Cotton and Coffee — The Native Country of the Coffee Shrub — First Use of Coffee in Europe — The Ancestor of all the American Coffee Shrubs — Comparative Value of Diamonds and Coffee, ... **157**

CHAPTER XI.
SELVAS OF THE AMAZONS.

Extent of the Selvas — Night in the Forest — Death-like Stillness — Roar of Wild Beast — Wild Chorus at Dawn — A Thunder Storm — A Primeval Forest and its Inhabitants — Large Locust Trees — Wonderful Fig-tree — Rosewood Trees, ... **163**

CHAPTER XII.
THE RIVER AMAZON, AND THE STORY OF MADAME GODIN DES ODONNAIS.

Course of the Amazon — Its Tributaries — Its Various Names — First Discovery — Expeditions of Orellana and Teixeira — Voyage of Madame Godin des Odonnais — Her Sufferings — Death of all her Companions — Ten days alone in the Forest — Her Meeting with the Indians — Arrival at Cayenne — Return to France, ... **175**

CHAPTER XIII.
PLANT AND ANIMAL LIFE ON THE AMAZON.

The Turtle of the Amazon — Turtle Egg Butter — Indian way of Catching Turtle — Indian Shooting — The Umbrella Bird — The Victoria Regia — The Jacana — The Fish Ox — The Anaconda — A Horse Swallowed by a Snake — Narrow Escape from a Boa Constrictor, ... **187**

CHAPTER XIV.
THE MINES OF UPPER PERU.

Situation and Productions of Bolivia — Maize — *Chicha* — *Quinoa* — *Coca* — Description of the *Coca* Bush — Cultivation and Uses — Silver Mines of Potosi — Discovery of the Mine, ... **204**

CHAPTER XV.

PERU.

Extent and Productions—Guano—Dangers of Travelling—Poisoned Springs — Storms among the Mountains — Peruvian Bridges — Encounter with a Tiger—Wonderful Escape, ... 214

THIRD DIVISION.

NORTHERN COUNTRIES.

| ECUADOR. | VENEZUELA. |
| NEW GRANADA. | GUIANA. |

CHAPTER XVI.

THE THREE REPUBLICS—ECUADOR, NEW GRANADA, AND VENEZUELA.

Description of the Country—Earthquakes—Productions—Pearl Fishery—Value of Pearls—Pearl Divers—Dangers and Labours of the Divers—A Shark Overhead, ... 222

CHAPTER XVII.

EARTHQUAKE IN QUITO.

Volcanoes near Quito—Desolation caused by them—Eruption of Cotopaxi — Story of a Sufferer — His Former Prosperity—A Sudden and Terrible Storm, ... 233

CHAPTER XVIII.

THREE DAYS IN A TREE.

The Extensive Plains called Llanos—The Plains on Fire—A Voyage on the Orinoco—A Night in a Mango Tree—Imprisoned in the Tree—Unpleasant Visitors—A Jaguar at the Foot of the Tree—A Fearful Conflict—The Fate of the Jaguar—Sufferings in the Tree—Despair—A Gleam of Hope—Deliverance, ... 238

CHAPTER XIX.

GUIANA.

Productions of Guiana—Population—British Guiana—French Guiana—Political Exiles in Guiana—Their Attempt to Escape—They Build a Raft—Their Sufferings—A Second Raft Built—A Perilous Voyage—The Exiles Reach a Dutch Colony, and are Kindly Received, 250

SOUTH AMERICA.

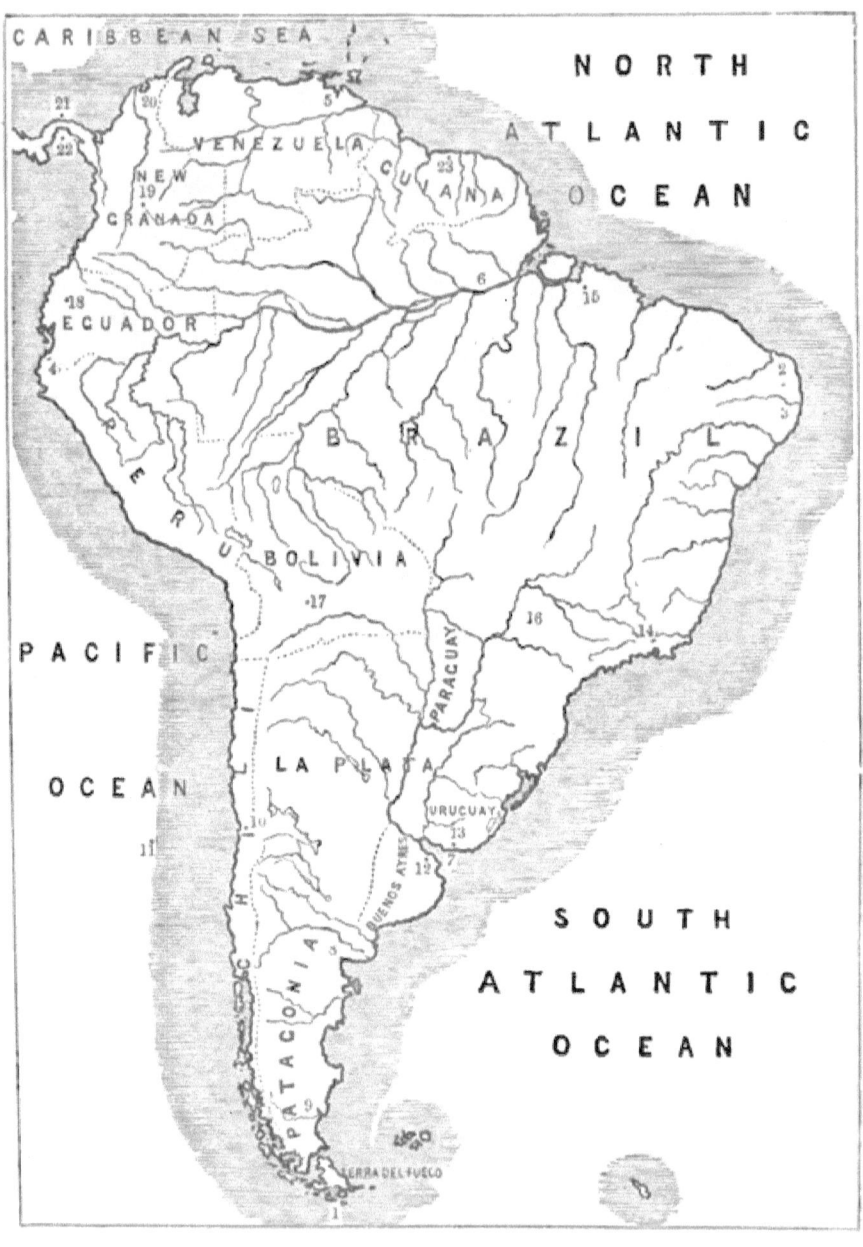

1. Cape Horn.
2. Cape St. Roque.
3. Cape St. Augustin.
4. Cape Blanco.
5. The Orinoco.
7. The Rio de la Plata.
8. The Rio Negro.
9. The Santa Cruz.
10. Valparaiso.
12. Buenos Ayres.
13. Monte Video.
14. Rio de Janeiro.
15. Para.
16. Minas Geraes.
18. Quito.
19. Santa Fe de Bogota.
20. Carthagena.
21. Portobello.
22. Panama.

PICTURES OF TRAVEL

IN FAR-OFF LANDS.

CHAPTER I.

TERRA DEL FUEGO.

General Description of the New World. Terra del Fuego—Cape Horn—Climate—Plants and Animals—People—Story of the Martyrs of Fuegia.

THE Continent of the New World consists of two great peninsulas, joined by a long narrow isthmus. It is 9000 miles long, extending from within the Arctic nearly to the Antarctic Circle. It is divided by nature into three parts—South, Central, and North America—and these three are connected by a mighty chain of mountains, called the Andes in South and Central America, and known as the Rocky Mountains in the North. It might seem almost as if the crust of the globe had been thinner, or had cracked and burst nearly in a line from north to south, and through this the mighty Andes had arisen, thrown up by the subterranean fires still burning so fiercely below them—ever and anon bursting forth afresh, and causing the earth to tremble and the hills to shake. And while the base of the mountains is thus plunged in the burning depths, their tops, often rising above the clouds, are covered with perpetual snow, while between every variety of climate may be found, according to the height to which you ascend.

"The greatest length of South America, from Cape Horn to the Isthmus of Panama, is about 4020 geographical miles. It is very narrow at its southern extremity, but increases in width northwards to the latitude of Cape San Roque, on the Atlantic; between which and Cape Blanco, on the Pacific, it attains its greatest breadth, of nearly 2750 miles. It consists of three mountain systems, separated by the basins of three of the greatest rivers in the world—the Orinoco, 1600 miles long; the Amazon or Maranon, about 4000 miles long; and the Rio de la Plata, 2700 miles long.

"The great chain of the Andes first raises its crest above the waves of the Antarctic Ocean, in the majestic, sombre mass of Cape Horn, the southernmost point of the archipelago of Terra del Fuego. This group of mountainous islands, equal in size to Great Britain, is separated from the mainland by the Strait of Magellan. The islands are penetrated in every direction by bays and narrow inlets of the sea, or fiords, ending often in glaciers fed by the snow on the summits of mountains 6000 feet high.

"From Cape Horn, the Andes runs along the western coast to the Isthmus of Panama, in a single chain of inconsiderable width, but majestic height, dipping rapidly to the narrow plains on the Pacific, but descending on the east by huge spires, or offsets, and deep valleys, to plains of vast extent, whose level is for hundreds of miles as unbroken as that of the ocean by which they are bounded. Nevertheless, two detached mountain systems rise from these plains—one in Brazil, between the Rio de la Plata and the river Amazon; the other, that of Parima and Guiana, between the river Amazon and the Orinoco."*

There are three great tracts of low lands in South America, known by the names of the Pampas, an Indian term, signifying flats, mostly treeless plains in the south, and covered with woods, swamps, and grassy fields in the north; the Selvas, or forest plains of the Amazon; and the Llanos, or level fields, chiefly covered with luxuriant grass. These plains and their inhabitants will be more minutely described in the course of the following chapters.

TERRA DEL FUEGO.

The outline of South America may be compared to a paper kite; and, like a kite, there is attached to its apex a jointed tail, of which Fuegia and the South Shetlands are the only fragments seen above water—in other words, the mighty wall of the Andes is broken through by the sea, and the inundated valley forms the Strait of Magellan; and after a feeble re-appearance in the Fuegian archipelago, the Cordillera is lost in the ocean.

As seen on a school-room map, this Terra del Fuego is a dim islet, deriving its chief importance from its famous headland, Cape Horn. On a nearer

---

* From "Memoir of Richard Williams," by Rev. Dr. Hamilton.

inspection, however, this nebulous patch resolves into a cluster of islands, one very large, with a crowd of smaller attendants to the west and south; and, far from the mainland, stands the kerbstone of the New World—Cape Horn, with his surf-beaten pyramid.

CAPE HORN.

Though only the fag-end of America—a mere caudal vertebra of the Andes—if we had it in Europe, Terra del Fuego would be a country of some consideration. Its second-rate islands are larger than the Isle of Wight or the Isle of Man.

and the surface of its mainland is equal to the Lowlands of Scotland. Its climate, however, renders it one of the most dreary and inhospitable regions on the face of the globe. In a latitude corresponding to Edinburgh, the sky seldom clears, and the rainy squalls of the summer are the only relief from the sleet and snow of the winter. A calm sunshine is a great rarity. If we imagined the mountains of the Hebrides rising to a height of six or seven thousand feet, with glaciers coming down to the sea, and a warm tide constantly flowing at their base; and if, moreover, we could bring the north Polar ice into as low a latitude as the Antarctic ice descends, our own Western Isles would be the counterpart of Fuegia.

The range between the extremes of heat and cold is small; and this comparative equability, along with the abundant moisture, is favourable to certain forms of vegetable life. In most districts of Britain, the fuchsia is a conservatory plant; but in Devonshire and the Isle of Bute it grows luxuriantly in the open air, and in winter wants no shelter. Fuegia is one of its native lands; and there, along with its equally delicate companion, *Veronica decussata*, it becomes a tree with a trunk half a foot in diameter. The potato is indigenous on the adjacent mainland, although we do not know that it has been found in these islands where celery, a kind of currant, the berry of an *arbutus*, and a *fungus*, are the only esculents. The characteristic vegetation is two sorts of beech-trees. One of these (*Fagus betuloides*) is an evergreen; the other (*Fagus Antarctica*) is deciduous. The latter species is more hardy, and can scale the mountain sides to a higher platform than its glossy-green companion; so that in winter a zone of leafless trees is seen at a lofty elevation, succeeding to the verdure of the forest. Except where discouraged by the thin, granitic soil, these beeches occur everywhere; and except when stunted by the winds, they attain a goodly size; and one trunk is mentioned seven feet in diameter.

Land animals are few; even insects are rare; the gloomy woods are inhabited by few birds. The most important quadruped is the guanaco, or llama, that useful compromise between the sheep and the camel, so characteristic of the South American mountains. It is found on Navarin island, and on the main island, or Terra del Fuego proper. Two species of fox, and a few mice and bats, complete the list of the land animals.

But the waters largely compensate for the lifelessness of the land. Seaweeds of gigantic size feed and shelter a great variety of molluscs and crustaceans. Shoals of fishes frequent the shore, and in the wake of the fishes come armies of seals and clouds of sea fowl.

The inhabitants of the Fuegian archipelago are closely allied to their neighbours the Patagonians, but are both intellectually and physically inferior to them. Their colour is something between dark copper and brown; Captain Fitzroy compares it to very old mahogany. But owing to the wood smoke with which they are saturated, the oil and blubber with which they are smeared, and the earth—white, red, and black—with which they are painted, it is difficult to ascertain a Fuegian complexion. Their

A SAVAGE LIFE. 19

FUEGIANS.

bodies and heads are large, their legs are crooked and stunted, their clothing is scanty, and nothing can be more wretched than their habitations. They live chiefly on fish and sea-fowl, when they can catch them; but for a great period of every year these poor islanders are entirely dependent on mussels, limpets, and similar shell-fish. Like most savages, the life of a Fuegian is an alternation of occasional feasts, with long intervals of famine. In the desperation of hunger, it is fearful to think of the expedients to which he is occasionally driven. There can be no doubt that these Indians are cannibals, and that when other subsistence fails, they kill and devour their old women before they kill their dogs. Those who fall in battle are in like manner devoured by the victors.

Degraded as the savages are, traces of gentleness and tenderness may be found among the women, but the mercies of the men are cruel. The men are surly tyrants, the women are laborious slaves. An incident, related by Commodore Byron, shows their almost incredible ferocity:—

"Our cacique and his wife had gone off in their canoe, when she dived for sea-eggs; but not meeting with great success, they returned a good deal out of humour. A little boy of theirs, about three years old, whom they appeared to be doatingly fond of, watching for his father and mother's return, ran into the surf to meet them; the father handed a basket of sea-eggs to the child, which being too heavy for him to carry, he let it fall; upon which the father jumped out of the canoe, and catching the boy up in his arms, dashed him with the utmost violence against the stones. The poor little creature lay motionless and bleeding, and in that condition was taken up by the mother; but died soon after. She appeared inconsolable for some time; but the brute, his father, showed little concern about it."

Embruted as are these savages, they are not sunk beyond recovery. Through the mercy of our God, there is at this moment on the earth a power well able to cure the worst woes of Fuegia.

THE MARTYRS OF FUEGIA.

Captain Gardiner, a Christian officer in the British navy, became deeply interested in the introduction of the gospel among the South American Indians. He found that little good could be done in the north, as the people were on every side so hemmed in by Spanish Popery. However, the regions in the south appeared more practicable. There were no Romish priests in Patagonia. Far away as Fuegia was, and few as were its hungry barbarians, he could plead their relative importance. Guiana excepted, of all that mighty continent, no other spot was accessible to Protestant missions. It was the Gibraltar of the South Pacific, and it was of no small consequence to our mariners, to people with friendly occupants the Straits of Magellan, and the coasts in the rear of Cape Horn. Above all, it was the only avenue attainable to the vast tribes of the interior, the tenants of the Andes, and the fierce nomads of the Pampas; and as Popery had closed the main gates against the gospel, it was of paramount urgency to seize and keep open this postern. After many fruitless attempts, the efforts of the earnest and heroic Captain Gardiner were at last successful in organising a mission.

Accompanied by Mr. Williams and Mr. Maidment, catechists, a ship carpenter, and three young seamen from Cornwall, he embarked in September 1850, on board a vessel named the " Ocean Queen," bound for San Francisco, California, which, on the 5th December of the same year, landed the little party on one of the islands of the Terra del Fuegian archipelago. They had taken with them two launches, twenty-six feet long, the one to be used as a floating mission-house, the other as a store ship and magazine, with two small boats as tenders, as Captain Gardiner's plan was to follow from island to island the migrations of the restless inhabitants, and also that in case the natives should prove unfriendly, the missionaries might be able to take shelter in their boats. On the 19th of December the "Ocean Queen" sailed on her voyage, leaving the small party alone.

A train of disasters soon overtook Gardiner and his companions. The launches were found unfit for the navigation of these stormy seas, and soon became leaky. The small boats and an anchor were lost; their gunpowder had been left in the "Ocean Queen." The natives, too, gave them great annoyance, being kept in good humour only by presents; and when these were refused, they seized every opportunity of purloining the mission property. One of their boats became a wreck, having been driven on the rocks. The party in this boat then took to a cavern; but finding it damp, and the tide washing into it, they hauled the wreck of the "Pioneer" (so the boat was named) on the beach, and, covering her with a tent, made a dormitory of her. Their health suffered from their continued hardships; their provisions began to fail; they were weakened both by disease and famine. Winter weather came on; snow fell day after day, covering all around with its white mantle, accompanied by fearful storms of wind. They tried in vain to catch fish,—none were to be seen; and the provisions they had brought with them were fast consuming away. Yet, amid all these outward hardships, their faith and patience failed not, and they enjoyed peace through the sustaining power of divine grace.

Some extracts from their journals may give an idea of what their sufferings were, and how patiently these were borne:—

"On Friday, May 2d, the captain and Mr. Maidment succeeded in catching a fox, or rather in killing him. He had frequently paid them visits during the night, entering the cavern whilst they were in bed in the boat, and making free with whatever came to hand. He had carried off pieces of pork, shoes, and even books; and, to the great mortification of Mr. Maidment, his Bible was among the latter, which, being bound in morocco, was doubtless a booty to the hungry beast. They therefore laid a bait for him,—a piece of pork attached by a cord to the trigger of a loaded gun, so placed that when he took the bait he should fire the gun. He fired it off once, but escaped unhurt; twice the cap went off, but the powder did not take fire. At last he received the whole discharge in his breast. In his stomach were found feathers, fish, and mice. He was a fine animal, with a splendid brush. Albeit the odium attached to a fox, our party on shore have already so far overcome any fastidiousness, that this morning they made a hearty breakfast of his 'pluck.' His quarters were cut up, and kept in reserve. This is not the first extraordinary *bonne bouche* our worthy caterer has put upon the spit, or made into soup for us. The penguin and shag, and the equally fishy-tasted duck, have all contributed their quota. The penguin was caught on shore, without attempting to get away, more than by a backward movement, as Mr. Maidment laid hold on him. The shag was asleep on a fallen tree lying on the beach, so that Mr. M. caught it also by hand.

"The most formidable drawback of all is the dampness of the boat. Although I have my Mackintosh spread over my bed, the water from the roof lodges in pools upon it, and has at length saturated the counterpane under it. The side of our beds, and all our clothes there, as well as at the head and the foot, are all wringing wet."

In the midst of sufferings such as these, from cold and wet, sickness, disease, and famine, the noble little band were still patient and resigned. On the 7th of May (eight months after they had left Liverpool) Mr. Williams thus writes:—

"Should anything prevent my ever adding to this, let my beloved ones at home rest assured that I was happy beyond expression the night I wrote these lines, and would not have changed situations with any man living. . . . The hope laid up for me in heaven filled my whole heart with joy and gladness. To me to live is Christ, to die is gain. I am in a strait betwixt two,—to abide in the body, or to depart and be with Christ, which is far better. Let them know that I loved them, and prayed *for every one* of them. God bless them all."

"*May* 20.—I am now, as it were, suspended by a slender thread betwixt life and death. Three days following I have had attacks which seemed to threaten a termination in dissolution. But God is with me. I am happy in the love of Christ. I could not choose, were it left to me, whether to die or to live."

" *May* 27.—To-day I have perceived new symptoms which show the inroads of the disease upon my system, and strongly point out a fatal termination. Can I be in any way disappointed at this, instead of a life of much service and glory to God? No, not for a moment; for God's glory can only be enhanced by fulfilling the counsels of his own will; and to suffer his blessed will as much glorifies my God as to do it. I am not disappointed; rather do I rejoice greatly that now it seems manifestly the design of God to take me hence. . . . Should this, then, be the will of God, then, my beloved ones, weep not for me. Let no mourning thought possess your hearts, nor sigh of sadness once escape your lips. Say rejoicingly, How good was the Lord! How greatly was he blessed of God; and he is gone to be with Jesus!"

Frequent mention is made in their journals of the tide washing into the cavern, carrying away their stores, and endangering their sleeping boat. This they endeavoured to counteract by building breakwaters of stones; but these were often washed away by the surf in the night. On one occasion Captain Gardiner and Mr. Maidment were obliged to escape from the cavern to save their lives; and taking refuge on a rock washed by the surf, they knelt down in prayer.

Early in June, their fishing-net had been swept away, which lessened their means of procuring food.

On the 28th of June, Captain Gardiner says: "Found Mr. Williams and Badcock to-day very ill Mr. W. considers the latter beyond the hope of recovery. He is most patient, leaning only upon his God. . . . Mr. Williams was praying aloud, when I reached the boat, for himself and his dying companions, committing themselves to God, and rejoicing in his faithfulness and truth."

At eleven o'clock on that same evening, John Badcock died. He requested Mr. Williams to join him in singing a hymn. He sang it through with a loud voice, and, a few minutes afterwards, expired. His companions buried him on a bank under the trees at Cook's river; and, after the sad funeral, they retired to their boat for prayers.

On the 4th of July, after having been for seven weeks on short allowance, their small rations were still more diminished. Everything in the shape of food was eagerly eaten, even a half-devoured fish washed up on the shore. Captain Gardiner writes: "We have now remaining half a duck, about one pound of salt pork, the same quantity of damaged tea, a very little rice (a pint), two cakes of chocolate, four pints of pease, to which I may add six mice. The mention of this last item in our list of provisions may startle some of our friends should it ever reach their ears; but circumstanced as we are, we partake of them with a relish, and have already eaten several of them; they are very tender, and taste like a rabbit."

July 22.—They were reduced to living on mussels, and the cravings of hunger were painfully felt. Captain Gardiner says: "After living on mussels for a fortnight, I was compelled to give them up, and my food is now mussel broth and the soft part of limpets."

July 28.—Captain Gardiner writes of the party in the other boat: "They are all extremely weak and helpless. Even their garden-seeds used for broths are now all out."

August 14.—Captain Gardiner is quite exhausted, and obliged to take to bed; but a rock-weed is discovered, which they boil to a jelly, and find nourishing.

August 23.—John Irwin died; three days after, John Bryant died also, and Mr. Maidment buried them both in one grave; and John Pearce, the remaining boatman, was so much grieved at the loss of his comrades, that his mind became wandering.

From Captain Gardiner's Journal, dated Wednesday, 3d September, the following is extracted:—

"Mr. Maidment returned (from burying his two companions) perfectly exhausted. The day also was bad,—snow, sleet, and rain. He has never since recruited from that day's bodily and mental exertion. Wishing, if possible, to spare him the trouble of attending on me, and for the mutual comfort of all, I purposed, if practicable, to go to the river and take up my quarters in the boat. This was attempted on Sunday last. Feeling that without crutches I could not possibly effect it, Mr. Maidment most kindly cut me a pair (two forked sticks); but it was with no slight exertion and fatigue in his weak state. We set out together; but soon found that I had no strength to proceed, and was obliged to return before reaching the brook over our own beach. Mr. Maidment was so exhausted yesterday, that he did not rise from his bed until noon, and I have not seen him since; consequently, I tasted nothing yesterday. I cannot leave the place where I am, and know not whether he is in the body, or enjoying the presence of the gracious God whom he has served so faithfully. I am writing this at ten o'clock in the forenoon. Blessed be my heavenly Father for the many mercies I enjoy,—a comfortable bed, no pain, nor even cravings of hunger, though excessively weak, scarcely able to turn in my bed—at least it is a very great exertion; but I am, by his abounding grace, kept in perfect peace, refreshed with a sense of my Saviour's love, and an assurance that all is wisely and mercifully appointed, and pray that I may receive the full blessing which it is doubtless designed to bestow. My care is all cast upon God; and I am only waiting his time and his good pleasure to dispose of me as he shall see fit. Whether I live or die, may it be in him. I commend my body and soul into his care and keeping; and earnestly pray that he will mercifully take my dear wife and children under the shadow of his wings,—comfort, guide, strengthen, and sanctify them wholly, that we may together, in a brighter and eternal world, praise and adore his goodness and grace in redeeming us with his precious blood, and plucking us as brands from the burning, to bestow upon us the adoption of children, and make us inheritors of his heavenly kingdom. Amen.

"*Thursday, September* 4.—There is now no room to doubt that my dear fellow-labourer has ceased from his earthly toils, and joined the company of the redeemed in the presence of the Lord, whom he served so faithfully. Under these circumstances, it was a merciful Providence that he left the boat, as I could not have removed the body. He had left a little peppermint-water, which he had mixed, and it has been a great comfort to me; but there was no other drink. Fearing I might suffer from thirst, I prayed that the Lord would strengthen me to procure some water. He graciously answered my petition; and yesterday I was enabled to get out, and scoop up a sufficient supply from some that trickled down the stern of the boat, by means of one of my India-rubber overshoes. What combined mercies am I receiving at the hands of my heavenly Father! Blessed be his holy name!

"*Friday*, September 5.—Great and marvellous are the loving-kindnesses of my gracious God unto me. He has preserved me hitherto, and for four days, although without bodily food, without any feeling of hunger or thirst."

The last remarks are not written so plainly as the previous day; yet they were not the last, for another paper, addressed to Mr. Williams by Captain Gardiner, was found, written in pencil, the whole being very indistinct, and some parts nearly obliterated, but nearly as follows:—

"My dear Mr. Williams,

"The Lord has seen fit to call home another of our little company. Our dear departed brother left the boat on Tuesday afternoon, and has not yet returned. Doubtless he is in the presence of his Redeemer, whom he served faithfully. Yet a little while, and though . . . . the Almighty to sing the praises . . . . throne. I neither hunger nor thirst, though . . . . days without food. . . . . Maidment's kindness to me . . . . heaven.

" Your affectionate brother in . . . .
"Allen F. Gardiner.
"*September* 6, 1851."

Meantime the sufferers were not forgotten. Their friends in England had been for some time vainly trying to get a vessel to convey stores to them, although far from aware of the extreme necessity of the case, as they hoped that fish and game might have furnished them with abundant supplies. At length, on the 21st of October, a pilot-boat, sent by Samuel Lafone, Esq., of Monte Video, reached Banner Cove, and finding the words painted on the rocks, "Gone to Spaniard Harbour," proceeded thither. They found a boat on the beach, and inside of it lay one person—dead. There was a large scar on his head, and another on his neck; and a mattress was thrown over him. The name "Pearce" was found on his frock; and there can be little doubt that he was the last survivor of the party. The Indians, whose naked footprints were observed on the strand, had no doubt found him still alive, and had murdered him; and books, papers, medicine—everything which was of no value to the savages—were found scattered on the deck, or strewn along the beach. On the shore was found a body completely washed to pieces, which must have been that of Mr. Williams, as his three companions had been already buried. Captain Smyley (the commander of the pilot-boat) had barely time to bury it, when a violent gale arose, and drove him from his anchorage and out to sea. His little vessel being laden with the crew of a castaway Danish bark, Captain Smyley could prosecute the search no further, but was forced to return to Monte Video.

Unapprised of Captain Smyley's discovery, Captain Morshead, in H.M.S. *Dido*, reached these dangerous seas about the middle of January **1852**. He had received instructions to touch at Picton Island, and inquire after the missionaries; and he prosecuted the search with the skill and energy of a British sailor, and with the solicitude of a Christian friend. He reached Spaniard Harbour on the evening of 21st January, and immediately sent Lieutenant Pigott and Mr. Roberts on shore. They found the bodies of Captain Gardiner and Mr. Maidment, and returned to the ship with a variety of books and papers. Next morning, amidst threatening weather, Captain Morshead landed. Mr. Maidment's body lay in the cavern where he had so often spent the night, and in which the stores rescued from the *Pioneer* were kept. Outside, on the rocks, was painted, by way of direction to any visitor, a hand, and under it, "Psalm lxii. 5–8." Captain Gardiner's body was found lying beside the wreck of the *Pioneer*. It seemed that he had left his berth, but, being too weak to climb into it again, he had died at the side of the boat. The remains were collected and buried, the funeral service was read, an inscription was placed on the rocks, three volleys of musketry were fired, the ship's colours were struck half-mast high, and, having fulfilled her mournful commission, the *Dido* went on her way.

May we not say of Captain Gardiner, as it was said of Abel, "he being dead yet speaketh" (Heb. xi. 4). Many lessons are taught us by the devotion and self-sacrifice of these noble martyrs of Fuegia. We see that in the most desolate situation the Christian need not fear, for the heavenly Comforter can inspire him with "joy unspeakable and full of glory," even in circumstances the most forlorn.

But besides their lesson of self-devotion, have not these good confessors left to the Church a legacy of duty? Have not their writings, so remarkably preserved, come back from the ends of the earth, as a cry to go over and help these poor degraded Indians?

This cry has not been unheard. Again a valiant band of Christian soldiers have gone forth prepared for the battle-field of these savage lands. The Patagonian Mission has been revived, and is now established on a firmer basis, and with fairer prospects, than ever. Captain Gardiner's suggestion of a mission ship has been adopted, and the "*Allen Gardiner*," with a mission family on board, is now his *floating* monument among those islands, the welfare of whose inhabitants lay so near his heart. His only son, Allen Gardiner, Esq., B.A. of Oxford, has accompanied the mission party as catechist, to aid in carrying out his father's plans.

Captain Gardiner has not lived in vain, neither died in vain, although we may not see the immediate fruits of his labours.

"THE LAND OF FIRE."*

Far, far away,
Over ocean's spray,
Where the billows roll,
By the icy Pole,
     Lies the "Land of Fire!"

What strange forms appear
Flitting here and there
Man! this is no other
Than thy heathen brother
     In the "Land of Fire!"

What so cold is known
As man's heart of stone,
Ere one beam from heaven
Warmth and light have given,
     Kindling Sacred Fire!

Though his heart be frozen,
He whom God hath chosen,
He the ice can melt—
Thousands this have felt
     With His Word of Fire!

Take that blessed Word,
Speak of Christ your Lord;
His all-powerful name,
Everywhere the same,
     Warms with heavenly Fire!

Not a moment burning,
Then to gloom returning;
Light that comes from Jesus,
Burns when all else freezes—
     'Tis a quenchless Fire!
         From the "Voice of Pity."

---

* Tierra del Fuego signifies "The Land of Fire."

CHAPTER II.

PATAGONIA.

Extent—Climate—Animals—People—Savage Life—Mode of Hunting—Marriage among the Patagonians—Adventures of Mr. Bourne, or "Life among the Giants."

The name of Patagonia has been given to the vast country which occupies the southern extremity of South America. It is about four times the size of Great Britain. The western part is traversed by the Andes; the eastern part is, for "800 miles, a desert of shingle, occasionally diversified by huge boulders, tufts of brown grass, low bushes armed with thorns, salt lakes and saline incrustations, as white as snow, and by black basaltic platforms, like plains of iron, at the foot of the Andes, barren as the rest." Eastern Patagonia is not, however, one universal flat, but a succession of shingly plains, rising in long low terraces to the foot of the Andes, here and there intersected at long distances by a ravine or a stream. Coarse wiry grass grows luxuriantly in the valleys; low thorny bushes, and underwood, are tolerably abundant; but nothing is to be seen in the plains worthy the name of a tree. They are bleak, barren, and desolate beyond description.

A BARREN REGION.

The climate is cold and severe; the icy winds from the Andes, or from the Pole, sweep over these inhospitable plains during the greater part of every year; yet the heat during the short summer is intense. The greatest misfortune of these regions is want of water. There are very few streams. Rain falls only in small quantity, and at rare intervals. The natives draw their supplies principally from springs

GUANACO.

or pools in the valleys, the water of which is generally brackish and disagreeable.

There are as few animals as plants. The guanaco,

a quadruped allied to the llama, is found in considerable numbers. It is larger than the red deer, very fleet, and is usually found in large herds. The guanaco furnishes most of the food of the Patagonians, and all their clothing. The skin also forms their tents, bridles, &c. The enemy of the guanaco is the cougar, or American lion, a small but ferocious creature. He is followed in the air by the hungry vulture, or condor of the Andes, which can scent a dead or dying animal from a great distance, and darts with the rapidity of lightning on the broken remains of the lion's feast.

Another remarkable bird, which roams over the Patagonian plains, is the cassowary, a species of ostrich smaller than that of Africa. Like the lion, it is smaller than its African namesake. Its flesh is tender and good, and is much prized by the Indians. It is exceedingly swift, often fleet enough to outstrip a good horse.

The inhabitants of Patagonia are savage Indians, so gigantic as to excite the wonder of the first travellers who saw them. Their height was exaggerated by report till they were magnified into giants, which is rather beyond the truth. They are, however, really of great stature; their average height is said, by Mr. Bourne (who lived long among them), to be about six feet and a half; and he saw several of them seven feet high. They wear large mantles of guanaco skins, sewed together with the sinews of the ostrich; and these fitting closely at the neck, and falling round them to below the knee, serve to increase their apparent height. Their long, thick, coarse hair hangs over their shoulders and back, giving them a wild fierce look. They have large heads, high cheek-bones, and their dark skins are usually painted with a motley mixture of colours, red, black, and white, in lines which cross the forehead in all directions, with white circles round the eyes.

CASSOWARY, OR AMERICAN OSTRICH.

They lead a wandering and wretched life; often suffering from hunger, dirty to a revolting degree, and actually gnawed by vermin. They eat any kind of meat they can get, but they prefer the flesh of the horse. The women are treated as slaves, as is the case among all savages; and, of course, they

EMBELLISHING NATURE.

A GROUP OF PATAGONIANS.

are degraded beings, although they possess the only virtue ever heard of in connection with these wild tribes,—they bear ill-treatment meekly. They are not beautiful by nature, and make themselves still more hideous by bedaubing themselves with a mixture of clay, blood, and grease.

skin of the guanaco, and are open on the east side. In the interior, nothing is to be seen except the skins on which they sleep, and their arms. The principal of these is the *bolas*, a missile weapon used in the capture of all kinds of game. This consists of two round stones, or lead balls, if they can be procured, weighing each about a pound, connected by a strap, or thong of leather, ten or twelve feet long. When engaged in the chase—his horse at the highest speed—the rider holds one ball in his hand, and whirls the other rapidly above his head; when it has acquired sufficient momentum, it is hurled with unerring aim at the object of pursuit, and either strikes the victim dead, or coils inextricably about him, and roots him to the spot, a helpless mark for the hunter's knife.

The hunting of the guanaco is not only the chief reliance for food of the native tribes, but is a spirited amusement, conducted after a fashion peculiar alike to hunters and hunted. Patagonia, as before mentioned, has no trees, but is covered here and there in patches, with a kind of underbrush of scrub growth; and the plains extend back for hundreds of miles from the Atlantic shore, like a vast rolling prairie. This affords a clear and excellent hunting-ground, with nothing to conceal the game, or hinder the pursuer, except now and then a clump of low bushes, or the tall grass of the marshes. Two to four hundred Indians, on horseback, bare-headed, and with their skin mantles about them, and each having the *bolas* and his long knife tucked beneath his belt, the whole followed by an innumerable pack of dogs of every kind, down to curs of low degree, make up a hunting party; as far as the eye can reach, their gigantic forms diminished by the distance, may be seen, projected on the horizon, their long hair streaming in the wind. Presently a thickness is perceived in the air, and a cloud of dust arises—a sure indication that a herd of guanacos has been beaten up, and is now approaching. All eyes are fixed intently on the cloud; it soon appears as if several acres of earth were alive, and in rapid motion. There is a herd of from five hundred to a thousand of these animals, infuriated, rushing forward at their utmost speed; whatever direction they may chance to take, they follow in a straight line, and as soon as their course is ascertained, the Indians may be seen running their horses at breakneck pace, to plant themselves directly in the course of the living tide. As the game approach, the hunter puts spurs to his horse and rushes across their track. When within twenty or thirty yards, he jerks the bolas from his girdle, and whirling it violently above his head, lets fly. The weapon usually strikes the head or neck of the animal, and winds itself about his fore-legs, bringing him to the ground. The hunter dismounts, cuts the victim's throat, remounts, and is again in pursuit. The whizzing missile, unerring in its aim, brings down another and another, till the party are satisfied with their chase and their prey. The dogs fall upon the poor animals, when helplessly entangled by the bolas, and often cruelly mangle them before the hunter has time to despatch them. Seldom does any one miss the game he marks. It is the height of manly ambition among them—the last result of

The sport being **over,** then comes the dressing of the meat. The **body is** split open, **the** entrails are removed, the heart **and** large veins opened, **to** permit the blood to flow into the **cavity.** The Indians scoop up with their hands, and eagerly drink the blood. When their thirst is satisfied, the remainder is poured into certain of the intestines selected for the purpose, to become (to their accommodating tastes) a luxury as highly prized as any surnamed of Bologna. The ribs are disjointed from the backbone, and with the head, are discarded as worthless. The body is quartered, cutting through **the** skin; the quarters, tied together in pairs, are thrown across the horses' backs, and conveyed to the camp. Arrived **at** their wigwams, **the** chivalrous hunters never unlade **their** beasts, **but** lean upon **the** horses' necks till their **wives come out** and relieve them of the spoil. They then dismount, unsaddle their horses, and turn them loose.

The only wealth of the Patagonians, except their huts, consists of horses, the stock of which **is** replenished by stealing from the Spanish and Chilian settlements. These animals are for the most part **of** inferior quality, though there are occasionally a **few** good ones among those which are stolen. There **are** rich and poor even among these savages; and riches and rank among them consist in being a *good thief*, and having plenty of horses. Mr. Bourne tells a most amusing story of an Indian who wished to marry the chief's daughter; but the father said: "**Indian** wants **a girl for his wife; poor** Indian— very poor, got no horses nor anything **else.** I won't give him the woman."

Mr. Bourne inquired the claims of the Indian: "What does poor Indian say?"

The reply was, "Says he'll steal plenty horses when we get where they are, and give the woman plenty of grease. Says he is a good hunter, good thief."

"Plenty of grease" seems to have been a bribe that the chief's daughter could not resist, and her mother pleaded her cause with the old chief, by saying that perhaps the Indian "might — who knew? — make a fine thief yet, and possess plenty of horses."

The girl and her mother prevailed, after the mother had borne a severe beating in the cause, and the promising thief became the chief's son-in-law. Such is a "marriage in high life" in Patagonia.

The degraded state of a people, among whom theft is held in honour, may easily be imagined. Mr. Bourne says that "the filth of their persons only too faithfully represents the degree in which 'their mind and conscience is defiled.'" Mind and body seem alike embruted.

Yet among these savages Mr. Bourne, an American, was long a captive—a fate so dreadful that we can only wonder he survived to relate his adventures, which are told in a most interesting book, entitled, "Life among the Giants," from which we extract the following story:—

LIFE AMONG THE GIANTS.

Soon after the discovery of gold in California, Mr. Bourne, among many others, embarked from

New Bedford, in the United States, on board a schooner bound for the gold regions. On account of the delays and dangers incident to doubling Cape Horn, the captain determined to attempt the passage of the Straits of Magellan. The vessel was becalmed off the mouth of the Straits, and a party was sent on shore for fresh provisions under the command of Mr. Bourne, who reluctantly went to oblige the captain.

By the treachery of the Indians, Mr. Bourne was separated from his men, and made prisoner. A gale came on, the ships were driven from their anchorage and carried out to sea, and Mr. Bourne was left alone in the power of his savage captors. His adventures are full of interest. We have space only for two scenes—his first repast in a Patagonian hut, and his escape.

When he first entered a Patagonian hut, he says that he felt "as bacon, if conscious, might be supposed to feel in the process of curing. No lapse of time," he continues, " was sufficient to reconcile my eyes, nostrils, and lungs to the nuisance. Often have I been more than half strangled by it, and compelled to lie with my face to the ground as the only endurable position. Talk that is 'worse than a smoky house,' must be something out of date, or Shakspeare's imagination never comprehended anything so detestable as a Patagonian hut. The chief and his numerous household, however, seemed to enjoy immense satisfaction; and jabbered, and grunted, and played their antics, and exchanged grimaces, as complacently as if they breathed a highly exhilarating atmosphere.

"My meditations and observations were shortly interrupted by preparations for a meal. My fancy began to conjure up visions of the beef, fowls, and eggs, the promise of which had lured my men from the boat, had proved stronger than the suggestions of prudence, and had made me a prisoner. But these dainties, if they existed anywhere within the old chief's jurisdiction, were just at present reserved. The old hag threw down from the top of one of the stakes that supported the tent the quarter of some animal, whether dog, guanaco, or whatever, was past imagining. She slashed right and left, might and main, with an old copper knife till the meat was divided into several pieces. Then taking a number of crotched sticks about two feet long, and sharpened at all their points, she inserted the forked ends into pieces of the meat, and drove the opposite points into the ground near the fire; which, though sufficient to smoke and comfortably *warm* the mess, was too feeble to roast it. At all events, time was too precious, or their unsophisticated appetites were too craving, to wait for such an operation; and the raw morsels were quickly snatched from the smoke, torn into bits by her dirty hands, and thrown upon the ground before us. The Indians seized them with avidity, and tossed a bit to me; but what could I do with it? I should have had no appetite for the dinner of an alderman at such a time and place, but as for tasting meat that came in such a questionable shape, there was no bringing my teeth and resolution to it. While eyeing it with ill-suppressed disgust, I observed the savages, like a horde of half-est relish. The old chief remarked the slight I was putting upon his hospitality, and broke in upon me with a fierce speech in his broken Spanish to this effect: 'Why don't you eat your meat? This meat very good to eat—very good to eat. Eat, man—eat!' Seeing him so much excited, and not knowing what deeds might follow his words if I refused, I thought it expedient to *try* to eat. I forced a morsel into my mouth. Its taste was by no means as offensive as its appearance had been unpromising, and I managed to save appearances with less disgust than I had feared. The eating being over, a large horn that had once adorned the head of a Spanish bullock was dipped into a leathern bucket and passed from one to another. Between the bucket and the horn, the water had gained a sickening taste; however, it seemed expedient 'to conquer my prejudices' so far as to drink with the other guests, and the ceremonies of dinner were over, for which I felt very thankful. Soon after, my painful thoughts were interrupted by an order to prepare for the night's repose. An old skin, about two and a half feet square, was thrown upon the cold ground in the back part of our rookery, and assigned for my couch. I took possession, and the whole family bestowed themselves in a row near me. The stifling atmosphere was soon vocal with their snoring."

Such was Mr. Bourne's first day among the savages, and his misery daily increased, his life was constantly in danger, while all attempts to escape proved vain. The Indians had learned a little Spanish, and Mr. Bourne also knew something of the language, and at first he communicated with them partly by means of this and partly by signs; but as he gradually learned to understand something of the native language, he began to promise them all manner of good things, especially rum and tobacco (the things most highly prized by savages), if they would take him to any place where there were white men. Moved by his bribes, the chief at last promised to take him to "Holland;" and the tribe accordingly set off on a journey northwards. He found that "Holland" was an island near the mouth of the river Santa Cruz. Mr. Bourne supposes that "Holland" might perhaps be the native corruption of the word "island." Several Europeans were living on the island, engaged in digging guano. The Indians hoisted a flag, stolen from an English ship, as a signal to induce the white men to come and trade with them, and Mr. Bourne resolved to make another attempt to escape. As he saw a hope of deliverance, his anxiety became intense. He says, "It was a season of deep, suppressed, silent misery, in which the heart found no relief but in mute supplication to Him who was alone able to deliver.

"There lay the little island—beautiful to eyes that longed, like mine, for a habitation of sympathising men—about a mile and a-half distant; it almost seemed to recede while I gazed, so low had my hope sunk under the pressure of disappointment and bitter uncertainty. A violent snow-storm soon setting in, it was hidden from view; everything seemed to be against me. It slackened, and partially cleared up; then came another gust, filling the air, and shutting up the prospect. In this way it continued till past noon; at intervals, as the sky lighted up, I took a firebrand, and set fire to the bushes on the beach, and then hoisted the flag again, walking wearily to and fro, till the storm ceased, and the sky became clear. The chief concealed himself in a clump of bushes, and sat watching, with cat-like vigilance, the movements of the islanders. After some time, he said a boat was coming. I scarcely durst look in the direction indicated, lest I should experience a fresh disappointment; but I did look, and saw, to my great joy, a boat launched, with four or five men on board, and pushing off the shore. On they came; the chief reported his discovery, and the rest of the Indians came to the beach, where I was still walking backward and forward. The boat approached, not directly off where I was, but an eighth of a mile, perhaps, to the windward, and there lay on her oars.

"The Indians hereupon ordered me to return to the camping-ground; but, without heeding them, I set off at a full run towards the boat. They hotly pursued, I occasionally turning and telling them to come on; I only wanted to see the boat. 'Stop, stop!' they bawled. 'Now, my legs,' said I, 'if ever you want to serve me, this is the time.' I had one advantage over my pursuers — my shoes, though much the worse for wear, protected my feet from the sharp stones, which cut theirs at every step; but, under all disadvantages, I found they made about equal speed with myself. As I gained a point opposite the boat, the Indians slackened their speed, and looked uneasily at me. The man in the stern of the boat hailed me, inquiring what Indians these were, what number of them, and how I came among them? I replied in as few words as possible, and told him we wished to cross to the island. He shook his head; they were bad fellows, he said; he could not take me with the Indians. They began to pull away. I made signs of distress, and waved them to return, shouting to them through my hands. The boat was again backed within hailing distance. 'Will you look out for me if I come by myself?' 'Yes,' was the prompt reply. The Indians, all this time, had kept within ten or fifteen feet of me, with their hands on their knives, and reiterating their commands to come back, at the same time edging towards me in a threatening manner. 'Yes, yes,' I told them, 'in a moment; but I wanted to look at the boat,' taking care, however, to make good my distance from them. At the same moment, I gave a plunge headlong into the river; my clothes and shoes encumbered me, and the surf, agitated by a high wind, rolled in heavy seas upon the shore. The boat was forty or fifty yards off; and as the wind did not blow square in-shore, drifted, so as to increase the original distance, unless counteracted by the crew. Whether the boat was backed up towards me, I could not determine; my head was a great part of the time under water, my eyes blinded with the surf, and most strenuous exertion was necessary to live in such a sea. As I approached the boat, I could see several guns pointed apparently at me. Perhaps we had misunderstood each other—perhaps they viewed me as an enemy! In fact, they were aimed to keep the

SAVED! SAVED! 49

ESCAPE OF MR. BOURNE.

Indians from following me into the water, which they did not attempt. My strength was fast failing me; the man at the helm, perceiving it, stretched out a rifle at arm's length. The muzzle dropped into the water, and arrested my feeble vision. Summoning all my remaining energy, I grasped it, and was drawn towards the boat. A sense of relief shot through and revived me, but revived also such a dread lest the Indians should give chase, that I begged them to pull away—I could hold on. The man reached down and seized me by the collar, and ordered his men to ply their oars. They had made but a few strokes, when a simultaneous cry broke from their lips, 'Pull the dear man in! pull the dear man in!' They let fall their oars, laid hold of me, and in their effort to drag me over the side of their whale-boat, I received some injury. I requested that they would let me help myself; and working my body up sufficiently to get one knee over the gunwale, I gave a spring, with what strength was left me, and fell into the bottom of the boat. They kindly offered to strip me, and put on dry clothes; but I told them, if they would only work the boat further from the shore, I would take care of myself. They pulled away, while I crawled forward, divested myself of my coat, and put on one belonging to one of the crew. Conversation, which was attempted, was impossible; it was one of the coldest days of a Patagonian winter. I was chilled through, and could only articulate, 'I can't talk now; I'll talk by-and-by.' Some liquor, bread, and tobacco, which had been put on board for my ransom, on supposition that this was what the signal meant, was produced for my refreshment. The sea was heavy, with a strong head-wind, so that, though the men toiled vigorously, our progress was slow. I was soon comfortably warmed by the stimulants provided, and offered to lend a hand at the oar, but the offer was declined. The shouts and screams of the Indians, which had followed me into the water, and rung hideously in my ears while struggling for life in the surf, were kept up till distance made them inaudible.

"The boat at last grounded on the northern shore of the island. Mr. Hall, the gentleman who commanded the party, supported my tottering frame in landing; and, as we stepped upon the shore, welcomed me to their island. I grasped his hand, and stammered my thanks for this deliverance, and lifted a tearful eye to heaven, in silent gratitude to God. I was then pointed to a cabin near by, where a comfortable fire was ready for me. 'Now,' I heard Mr. Hall say, 'let us fire a salute of welcome to the stranger. Make ready—present—fire!' Off went all their muskets, and a very cordial salute it appeared to be. He soon followed me, took me to his own dwelling, supplied me with dry clothing, and, above all, warmed me in the kindly glow of as generous a heart as ever beat in human bosom.

"I was captured by the savages on the 1st of May, and landed upon the island on the 7th of August.

"I passed, in the society of my deliverers, one of the happiest evenings of my whole life. The change was so great from the miserable and almost hopeless existence I had so long lived, that my joy exceeded all bounds. My heart overflowed with gratitude. Words could not then, and cannot now, convey any adequate impression of my feelings—of the freedom and joy that animated me on being snatched from perils, privations, and enemies, and placed, as in a moment, in security, in plenty, and in the society of friends."

The name of the island to which Mr. Bourne

escaped is Sea Lion Island. He remained there some months, and then embarked on board an American whaler. He afterwards visited California, and finally returned in safety to New York, after many strange and interesting adventures in various countries. He says, " The steamer, *State of Maine*, bore me to my home, January 13, 1852—after an absence of three years lacking a month—with a heart rising gratefully to God for his many interpositions in my behalf, to deliver me from the perils of the sea and the perils of the land."

CHAPTER III.

CHILI AND ITS ISLANDS.

Description of Chili—Its Mines—Animals—People—Conquest by the Spaniards—The Islands of Chili—Juan Fernandez—Adventures of Alexander Selkirk, the real "Robinson Crusoe."

If you cast your eyes on a map of South America, you will see, between the high mountain chain of the Andes or Cordilleras and the ocean, a long, narrow slip of land, hilly, volcanic, but well watered. This slip of land is Chili. It is favoured with one of the finest and healthiest climates in the world. As it is situated on the opposite side of the equator from us, it is summer there when we have winter, and its spring corresponds in time with our autumn. The soil is wonderfully fertile; and the productions of both hemispheres seem to thrive equally well there. In the interior, the corn sown often produces a hundred-fold, and maize is not less productive. Peaches grow to the weight of a pound, and apples may sometimes be seen as large as a person's head. The best kinds of strawberries grow in such profusion that this delicious fruit is often called in America "the fruit of Chili." Chili is almost the only country in the New World where the grapes yield good wine. Its forests are magnificent, and furnish many beautiful varieties of wood. The grass in its rich meadow pastures is often so tall and luxuriant as to hide the cattle grazing on it.

Chili also possesses valuable mines of gold and silver. The excellent copper which comes from the mines of Coquimbo is much esteemed in Europe; and there are several mines of coal which are now of great service.

CONDOR OF THE ANDES.

There are no dangerous animals to be feared in this highly favoured country; but the condor, the most powerful of the birds of prey, builds its nest on the summits of the Andes. In the same mountains, on the boundary between the inhabited part of the country and the snow line, live the vicuñas —beautiful quadrupeds of the same species as the llamas, whose fine wool is used in the manufacture of the most delicate stuffs and the softest cloths. Of the animals which furnish fur, the chinchilla, a small grey creature, with long, soft hair, is the best known and the most valued.

THE CHINCHILLA.

The people of Chili are partly whites of Spanish origin, along with a considerable number of Indians and half-bloods—all Papists. The Chilians of white descent are tall and strong, more active than creoles usually are; lovers of liberty; and more civilized in some respects than the other Spanish Americans. As to the natives, the bravery with which they defended their liberties when the country was subdued was the cause of their obtaining better conditions than the other conquered people; and they have always been better treated than the natives of the other provinces.

The ferocious Almagro, the companion and rival of Pizarro, the conqueror of Peru, was the first European who tried to take possession of Chili in 1535; but he soon left it, and was succeeded in the attempt by Valdivia in 1541. The war lasted ten years without intermission, and the Indians persevered in maintaining their independence, although constantly losing ground. An Indian chief, who was so bowed down with old age and infirmity that he was unable to leave his hut, heard those around him continually relating some fresh losses and misfortunes which were constantly occurring. The bitter grief of hearing that his countrymen were continually being defeated by a mere handful of strangers seemed to give new strength to the old man. He was inspired with fresh vigour, left his quiet hut, succeeded in raising thirteen regiments of a thousand men each, which he placed one behind the other, and led them against the enemy. If the first division should be routed, the men had orders not to fall back on the second division, but to try to rally behind the last. These orders, which were faithfully obeyed, disconcerted the Spaniards. They broke through division after division, yet seemed to gain no advantage. At length, both men and horses having great need of rest, Valdivia ordered his troops to retreat to a narrow defile, where he thought he might take up a position which would be easily defended. But he was not even permitted to reach it. The rearguard of the Indians had been before him. They had gone by a circuitous route and seized the pass, while the vanguard of the Indian army followed and watched the Spanish troops. Thus Valdivia was surrounded and massacred with the hundred and fifty men who composed his troop. It is said that the Indians poured melted gold down his throat. "Drink plentifully of the metal for which you have thirsted so greedily!" said these savages to their conquered enemy.

They took advantage of their victory to carry fire and desolation into the European settlements, of which they destroyed several. All would have shared the same fate, if a considerable reinforcement of troops, which arrived from Peru, had not enabled the Spaniards to defend their best fortified posts.

At a later period, the conquest of the country was again attempted by the Spaniards, and this time with success; but in no country did they meet with such obstinate resistance: and nowhere were they obliged to take so many precautions not to offend their new subjects, in case of driving them to join the Indian tribes which still continued independent.

The most celebrated of these Indian tribes are the Araucanian, who still preserve their freedom among their native mountains. They are brave and intelligent men, who live in large villages under settled laws and a regular government. Proud, industrious, and courageous, they are reckoned the most civilized of any of the native races of the New

World. They have not only skilful smiths and carpenters among them, but even jewellers, surgeons, physicians, and poets. Some of them are occupied with agriculture; but their chief riches consist in their flocks and herds. They have very numerous herds of horses and oxen, and they do not hesitate to add to them by making armed incursions into the territory of Chili, and carrying off as many as they can.

Chili is now a prosperous republic, containing about a million and a half of inhabitants. Its principal cities are San Jago (St. James), the capital, containing about seventy thousand inhabitants; and its sea-port, Valparaiso, which is one of the most important commercial places on the western coast of America. The sea-port towns of Coquimbo, Conception, and Valdivia also export many of the productions of the country.

The large island of Chiloé is attached to the republic of Chili. It is situated near the coast further to the south. It is damp and foggy, but fertile, and is inhabited chiefly by whites. The two celebrated islets called Juan Fernandez also belong to Chili. They are situated in the wide ocean, two hundred leagues from the coast of Chili, and are the penal settlements of the republic—unimportant in themselves, yet famous as the scene of the "Adventures of Robinson Crusoe," a book well known to every one.

In 1572, Juan Fernandez, a Spanish seaman, who often sailed between Peru and Chili, rightly calculated that, by keeping far out to sea, he would escape the contrary winds which often delayed his voyage along the coast; and by thus going out of the usual track, he discovered the island which bears his name. It is called by the Chilians *Mas-a-Tierra* (the nearest the land), as distinguished from the smaller islet near it, which they have named *Mas-a-Fuera* (the furthest off). Fernandez got a grant of the island which he discovered, and went to settle there, accompanied by a few families; but in a very short time these colonists, either discouraged by the want of communication with others, or from some other cause, abandoned the island, leaving no trace of their residence there, except a few goats, which increased in number to such a degree, that ships which passed near these shores occasionally touched at the island to supply themselves with water and goats' flesh. A few rats escaped from the ships, and several cats, which had been forgotten or left upon the island, considerably increased its animal population.

The island, usually called Juan Fernandez, is of an irregular form, approaching to a triangle, and is about five leagues in length, from north-west to south-east, and not more than two at its extreme breadth. The north-east side consists of lofty mountains and deep valleys, which are covered with trees and verdure. The middle of the island is so high, as to be almost inaccessible; the western end presents a loose, dry, stony, barren soil—all the harbours are on the north-east side.

Seen from a distance, the island resembles an immense mass of rugged mountains and rocks of the most forbidding aspect; but as you approach nearer, it assumes a more pleasing appearance, and the eye rests with delight upon the lofty eminences covered with wood, and here and there intersected by valleys. These are clothed in the most beautiful verdure, watered by numerous streams, which descend from rock to rock in *cascades*, or glide along among the underwood in silent loveliness.

Many of the mountains on the north-east side are inaccessible, but they are in general covered with wood. They run across the island from the north-west to the southern side, in which last the trees are not so numerous, being checked in their growth by the violence of the wind. Many of the mountains rise to a great height, and are overspread with a dense fog, especially in the morning and evening. The island is subject to sudden gusts of wind, which rush through the valleys into the bays with great violence; but they seldom last above two or three minutes. The air is in general mild, and the sky serene. During the summer months the heat is moderate. In the beginning of June, the winter sets in commonly with a northerly wind, and continues until the end of July, but it is not severe. In the worst days there is only a little frost, accompanied with hail; but there are occasionally heavy rains. The water is excellent; the soil upon the hills and in the valleys is a deep rich mould, and very fertile. All sorts of European and American corn, fruit, and quadrupeds, succeed extremely well, and the sea which washes the shores abound in fish.

The coast affords an abundance of seals and sea lions; but there are no native quadrupeds—the goats which, in the time of Selkirk's residence on the island, were so numerous, having been brought to it by the first discoverers.

The ornithology of the island is confined to the albatross, hawk, **oil**, pintado, a small humming-bird, and the pardela: this last **burrows** like a rabbit, rendering the ground unsafe to walk upon; remains torpid in the winter months; feeds on fish; and has **a** note, which it utters in the evening, resembling " Be quiet."

There are spiders, which make strong webs be-**tween the trees;** but no venomous creature is found on the island. A great variety of fish abound on the coasts.

The trees are palm, cabbage, malagita, pimento, Guinea pepper, black plums, cotton-trees, Italian laurels, myrtles, and **mountain ash. The** cotton-trees grow **to the** height **of twenty** yards, **and** planks **of forty feet in** length can **be** obtained from the myrtles.

The vegetables are a long grass, about the height of a man, that covers all the fertile parts of the island, very like oats; water-cresses, wild sorrel, fern, **clover,** wild oats, sour-docks, sow-thistles, mallows, wood-cresses, dandelion, night-shade; also pumpkins, Sicilian radishes, parsnips, turnips, parsley, purslain, and **a** herb that grows by the water-side, useful in fomentations, resembling fever-fern.

STORY OF ALEXANDER SELKIRK.

The island **of Juan** Fernandez was for **a** long **time a** regular resort of the Bucaneers, and was **also** often visited **by** ships **of** various nations. During the Spanish succession **war,** the crew of an English privateer, equipped **to** capture Spanish ships, remained there some months to supply themselves with fresh provisions and water. One of the men on board, named Alexander Selkirk, a Scotchman, having quarrelled with the captain, resolved to leave the ship and remain upon the island. Just before the ship sailed, he was landed with all his effects, which were his chest, containing his clothes, and a quantity of linen; his musket, which he afterwards brought home with him; a pound of powder, and balls in proportion; a hatchet and some tools; a knife; a pewter kettle; his flip-can, which he conveyed to Scotland (at present in the possession of John Selkirk, his great-grand-nephew); a few pounds of tobacco; the Holy Bible; some good books, and one or two works on navigation, with his mathematical instruments. He leaped on shore with a faint sensation of freedom and joy. He shook hands with his comrades, and bade them adieu in a hearty manner, while Stradling sat in the boat, urging their return to the ship, which order they instantly obeyed; but no sooner did the sound of their oars, as they left the beach, fall on his ears, than the horrors of being left alone—cut off from all human society, perhaps for ever—rushed upon his mind. His heart sunk within him, and all his resolution failed. He rushed into the water, and implored them to return and take him on board with them. To all his entreaties Stradling turned a deaf ear, and even mocked his despair; denouncing the choice he had made of remaining upon the island as rank mutiny, and describing his present situation as the most proper state for such a fellow, where his example

THE CASTAWAY.   63

For many days after being left alone, Selkirk was
under such great dejection of mind that he never
tasted food until urged by extreme hunger, nor did
he go to sleep until he could watch no longer; but
sat with his eyes fixed in the direction where he
had seen his shipmates depart, fondly hoping that
they would return and free him from his misery.
Thus he remained seated upon his chest until

ALEXANDER SELKIRK'S DESPAIR.

darkness shut out every object from his sight. Then
did he close his weary eyes; but not in sleep, for
morning still found him anxiously hoping the return
of the vessel.

When urged by hunger, he fed upon seals and
such shell-fish as he could pick up along the shore.

The reason of this was the aversion he felt to leave the beach, and the care he took to save his powder. Though seals and shell-fish were but sorry fare, his greatest inconvenience was the want of salt and bread, which made him loathe his food until reconciled to it by long use.

He was so miserable in his solitude, that at first he made no effort to improve his situation by making himself more comfortable. The beauty of the island was quite disregarded, and his time was spent watching the ocean, with the hope of seeing a sail appear in the distance. If we think for a moment how disagreeable it is to most men to be left by themselves even for a few days, we may form a faint idea of his situation, and how painful it must have been to him, a sailor, accustomed to enjoy and perform all the offices of life in the midst of bustle and fellowship. It was with difficulty he could bear the horror of being left in such a desolate place; and he became so melancholy, that he was nearly sinking into utter despair.

It was then, in the depths of his misery, when every other hope and comfort was gone, that the inestimable blessing of a religious education was felt in all its power. Alexander Selkirk was a Scotchman, a native of the little village of Largo in Fife, where he was born in the year 1676. He was one of a pious family, and had been very carefully instructed in his youth, although for a long time the teaching seemed thrown away. His father, a religious and very strict man, an elder in the church, attempted to control the wild, wayward spirit of his son; but his care was in a great degree counteracted by the mistaken indulgence of a weak mother, who tried to **conceal his** faults from his father. **In the** records of his early life we read **of constant** disputes between **him and** his brothers, which got to such a height that the elders of the **church** were obliged to take **up** the cause, and cite him before them. The records of the session of Largo record **the** fact of his appearance before **the** pulpit, when "he acknowledged his sin in disagreeing with his brothers, and was rebuked in the face of the congregation for it; and promised amendment, in the strength of **the** Lord, and so was dismissed." His promises were not **kept; and at last** casting off all authority, **and in** disobedience to his father's command, **he went off to sea.** Suffering was needed **to** tame **his** rebellious spirit, and it was **a suitable** punishment **for** the quarrelsome brother **and** disobedient son, who had despised the pleasures of a quiet home and his natural friends, to be left thus alone and desolate, without **a** human voice to cheer his dismal solitude. When misery had subdued the pride of his hard and stubborn heart, he turned **to God** against whom **he had** rebelled, **of** whom he had thought so little. His Bible was **in** his chest — probably put there **by** his pious parents' care — and he now began to study it, and to remember the lessons of his early years. **The** darkness of the despair that had nearly overwhelmed him began to clear away. By slow degrees he became submissive, resigned, and even cheerful; and began to do what he could to improve his condition.

The building of **a** hut was the first object that

roused him to exertion; and his necessary absence from the shore gradually weaned his heart from that aim which had alone absorbed all his thoughts, and proved a secondary means of his obtaining that serenity of mind he afterwards enjoyed; but it was eighteen months before he became fully composed, or could be for one whole day absent from the beach, and from his usual hopeless watch for some vessel to relieve him from his melancholy situation.

During his stay he built himself two huts, with the wood of the pimento-tree, and thatched them with a species of grass that grows to the height of seven or eight feet upon the plains and smaller hills, and produces straw resembling that of oats. The one was much larger than the other, and situated near a spacious wood. This he made his sleeping-room, spreading the bed-clothes he had brought on shore with him upon a frame of his own construction; and as these wore out, or were used for other purposes, he supplied their place with goats' skins. His pimento bed-room he used also as his chapel, for here he kept up that simple, but beautiful form of family worship which he had been accustomed to in his father's house. Soon after he left his bed, and before he commenced the duties of the day he sung a psalm or part of one, then he read a portion of Scripture, and finished with devout prayer. In the evening, before he retired to rest, the same duties were performed. His devotions he repeated aloud, to retain the use of speech, and for the satisfaction man feels in hearing the human voice, even when it is only his own. To distinguish the **Sabbath, he kept an** exact account of the days of every **week** and month during **the** time he remained upon the island, although **the** method he **adopted** is not mentioned **in** any document we have procured.

The smaller hut, which Selkirk had erected at **some** distance from the other, was used by him **as** a kitchen, **in which he dressed** his victuals. **The** furniture **was** very scanty, but consisted **of every** convenience his island could afford. His most valuable article was the pot or kettle he had brought from the ship to boil his **meat in; the spit was** his own handiwork, **made of such wood as** grew upon the island; **the rest was suitable to** his rudely-constructed habitation. Around **his** dwelling browsed **a** number of goats, remarkably tame, which **he** had taken when young, and lamed; **but** so as not to injure their health, while he diminished their speed. These he kept as a store, in the event of sickness or any accident befalling him that might prevent him from catching others; his sole method of **doing which** was running **them** down **by** speed **of foot.** The pimento-wood, which **burns** very bright and clear, served him both for fuel **and** candle. **It gives out an** agreeable **perfume while** burning.

He obtained fire after the Indian method, **by** rubbing two pieces of pimento-wood together until they ignited. This he did, as being ill able to spare **any** of his linen for tinder, time being of no value to him, and the labour rather **an** amusement. Having recovered his peace of mind, he found out new comforts, and was continually gaining some new acquisition to his store; he began likewise to enjoy greater variety in his food. The crawfish, many of which weighed eight or nine pounds, he broiled or boiled as his fancy led; seasoning it with pimento (Jamaica pepper); and at length he came to relish his food without salt.

As a substitute for bread, he used the cabbage-palm, which abounded in the island; turnips, or their tops; and likewise a species of parsnip, of good taste and flavour. He had also Sicilian radishes and water-cresses, which he found in the neighbouring brooks; as well as many other vegetables peculiar to the country, which he ate with his fish or goats' flesh.

Having food in abundance, and the climate being healthy and pleasant, in about eighteen months he became reconciled to his situation. The time no longer hung heavy on his hands. His devotions, and frequent study of the Scripture, soothed and elevated his mind; and this, coupled with the vigour of his health, and a constantly serene sky and temperate air, made his life a happy one. He took delight in everything around him; ornamented the hut in which he lay with fragrant branches, cut from a spacious wood, on the side of which it was situated; and so made a pleasant bower, in which he rested when tired with hunting.

During the early part of his residence, he was much annoyed by multitudes of rats, which gnawed his feet and other parts of his body as he slept during the night. To remedy this disagreeable annoyance, he caught and tamed, after much exertion and patient perseverance, some of the cats that ran wild on the island. **These new** friends soon **put** the rats to flight, and became themselves the companions of his leisure hours. He amused himself by teaching them to dance, and **do a** number of antic feats. **Their numbers** increased **so** fast, **too, under his** fostering hand, that they lay upon **his bed and upon** the floor in great numbers.

The island abounded **in** goats, which he shot while his powder lasted, and afterwards caught by speed of foot. At first he could only overtake kids; but his frugal life, with air and exercise, **so** improved his health and strength, **that** he could **at** length run down the **strongest goat on** the island. It was his custom, **after running down the** animals, to slit their ears, **and then** allow them to escape. **The** young he carried **to** the green lawn beside his hut, and employed his leisure hours in taming them. They, in time, supplied him with milk, and even with amusement, as he taught them, as well as his cats, **to dance;** and he often declared that **he never** danced with **a** lighter heart **or** greater spirit anywhere, **to** the best **of** music, than he did to the sound **of** his own voice, **with** his dumb companions. On one occasion, when pursuing a goat, he made a snatch at it **on the** brink **of** a precipice, of which he was not aware, as some bushes concealed it from him. The animal suddenly stopped; upon which he stretched forward his hands to seize it, when the branches gave way, **and** they both fell from a great height. Selkirk was **so** stunned and bruised by the fall, that he lay deprived of sensation and almost of life. **Upon** his recovery, he

ALEXANDER SELKIRK.

found the goat lying dead beneath him. This happened about a mile from his hut. Scarcely was he able to crawl to it when restored to his senses; and dreadful were his sufferings during the first two or three of the ten days that he was confined by the injury. He lay stretched upon his bed,

A RUDE ATTIRE.

unable to move but with extreme pain. There was no human being to reach him a drink of cold water, or to do the smallest service for him; yet he did not despair; his heart was at ease, and he poured it forth in prayer; he felt a peace of mind which religion can alone bestow; and even in this forlorn and painful situation, a ray of hope enlivened the gloom with which he was surrounded. This was the only disagreeable accident that befell him during his long residence on the island.

As to his clothing, it was very rude—shoes he had none,—for they had been soon worn out. This gave him very little concern, and he never troubled himself in contriving any substitute to supply their place. As his other clothes wore out, he dried the skins of the goats he had killed, to make them into garments, sowing them with slender thongs of leather, which he cut for the purpose, and using a sharp nail for a needle. In this way he made for himself a cap, jacket, and short breeches. The hair being retained upon the skin, gave him a very uncouth appearance; but in this dress he ran through the underwood, and received as little injury as the animal he pursued. Having linen cloth with him, he made it into shirts, sewing them by means of a nail, and the threads of his worsted stockings, which he untwisted for that purpose.

One day, in his ramble along the beach, he found a few iron hoops, which had been left by some vessel as unworthy to be taken away. This was to him a discovery that imparted more joy than if he had found a treasure of gold and silver, for with them he made knives when his own was worn out;

and bad as they were, they stood him in great stead. One of them, which he had used as a chopper, was about two feet in length, and was afterwards long kept as a curiosity at the Golden Head Coffee-house, near Buckingham Gate. It had been then changed from its original simple form, having, when last seen, a buckhorn handle, with some verses upon it.

Notwithstanding the tranquillity and peace of mind which he now enjoyed, he still anxiously looked out for a sail. The love of home was strong within him, and he longed for the means of returning. He was obliged, however, to be very cautious in observing the vessels that approached the island, to see whether they were English or foreign ships, as to have been taken by the Spaniards would have been certain misery. He chose rather to stay upon the island, and run the risk of dying alone, than fall into their hands, as they would either have murdered him in cold blood, or caused him to linger out a life of misery in the mines of Peru or Mexico, unless he chose to deny his religion and turn Papist; and even in that case he would have been compelled to renounce his country, and pass his weary days on board one of their coasting vessels; for it was one of their maxims never to allow an Englishman to return to Europe who had gained any knowledge of the South Seas. On one occasion Selkirk was very nearly caught by the crew of a Spanish ship which had anchored near the island. He was pursued, and several shots were fired in the direction in which he fled; and he narrowly escaped by getting up a tree, and remaining hid among the branches.

This adventure made him very cautious in venturing near the shore when strange ships were in sight.

At length, after he had been about four years on the island, two English vessels appeared on its coast. They were armed ships, named the *Duke* and the *Duchess*, fitted out to cruise against the French and Spaniards. **On** the 31st of January 1709, they came in sight **of** Alexander Selkirk's dominions, when he **was**, as usual, anxiously surveying the watery waste. Slowly the vessels rose into view; and he could scarcely believe the sight real, for often had he been deceived before. They gradually approached the island; and he at length ascertained them to be English. **Great was** the tumult of passions that rose **in his mind; but the love of** home overpowered them all. **It was late in** the afternoon when they first came in sight; and lest they should sail again without knowing that there was a person on the island, he prepared a quantity of wood to burn as soon as it was dark. He kept his eye fixed upon them till night fell, and then kindled his fire, and kept it up till morning dawned. His hopes and fears having banished all desire **for** sleep, he employed himself in killing several goats, and in preparing an entertainment for his expected guests, knowing how acceptable it would be to them after their long run, with nothing but salt provisions to live upon.

His fire had been seen by **those** in the ships, and had caused great surprise, **as** they supposed the island to be uninhabited; and next **day a** boat was **sent** on shore, with Captain Dover, Mr. Fry, and six men, all well armed, **to** ascertain the cause of the fire. Alexander saw the boat leave the *Duke*, and pull for the beach. He ran down joyfully to meet his countrymen, and to hear once more the human voice. He took in his hand a piece of linen tied upon a small pole as a flag, which he waved as they drew near to attract their attention. At length he heard them call to him, inquiring for a good place to land, which he pointed out; and flying as swift as a deer towards it, arrived first, where he stood ready to receive them as they stepped on shore. He embraced them by turns; but his joy was too great for utterance, while their astonishment at his uncouth appearance struck them dumb. He had at this time his last shirt upon his back; his feet and legs were bare; his thighs and body covered with the skins of animals. His beard, which had not been shaved for four years and four months, was of great length, while a rough goat's-skin cap covered his head. He appeared to them as wild as the original owners of the skin which he wore. At length they began to converse, and he invited them to his hut; but its access was so very difficult and intricate, that only Captain Fry accompanied him over the rocks which led to it. When Alexander had entertained him in the best manner he could, they returned to the boat, our hero bearing a quantity of his roasted goat's-flesh for the refreshment of the crew. During their repast, he gave them an account of his adventures and stay upon the island, at which they were much surprised.

In the afternoon the ships were cleared, the sails bent and taken on shore to be mended, and to make tents for the sick men. Selkirk's strength and vigour were of great service to them. He caught two goats in the afternoon. They sent along with him their swiftest runners and a bull-dog; but these he soon left far behind, and tired out. He himself, to the astonishment of the whole crew, brought the two goats upon his back to the tents.

The two captains remained at the island until the 12th of the month, busy refitting their ships, and getting on board what stores they could obtain. During these ten days, Alexander was the huntsman, and procured them fresh meat. At length, all being ready, they set sail, when a new series of difficulties of another kind annoyed Selkirk, similar to those he had felt at his arrival upon the island. The salt food he could not relish for a long time, having so long discontinued the use of it; for which reason he lived upon biscuit and water. Spirits he did not like from the same cause; and besides, he was afraid of falling into intemperance, for his religious impressions were as yet strong. From the confirmed habit of living alone, he was reserved and taciturn. This frame of mind, and a sedate expression of countenance, continued longer than could have been expected. Even for some time after his return to England these qualities were remarkable, and drew the notice of those to whose company he was introduced. Shoes gave him great inconvenience when he first came on board. He had been so long without them, that they made his feet swell, and crippled his movements; but this wore off by degrees, and he became once more reconciled to their use. In other respects, he gradually resumed his old habits as a seaman, but without the vices which sometimes attach to the profession. He rigidly abstained from profane oaths, and was much respected by both captains, as well on account of his singular adventures as of his skill and good conduct; for, having had his books with him, he had improved himself much in navigation during his solitude.

Alexander Selkirk continued with the ships during their cruise, and returned with them to England in the year 1711. On their return, they sailed round the east coast of Scotland, that country so dear to Selkirk, which at one time he had despaired of ever seeing again. His joy was extreme at the sight of the coast; and it was with a feeling of great pain that he saw it disappear from his sight without being permitted to land. When he arrived in London, he had been eight years, one month, and three days absent from his native country. His adventures excited great interest in London, and made his company be courted by the curious and the learned; but his earnest desire was to return home; and as soon as he had realised the proceeds of his voyage, he set out for Largo, his native village. It was the forenoon of the Sabbath-day, when all were in church, that he knocked at the door of his father's house, but found not those whom he so earnestly longed to see. He set out for the church, prompted both by his piety and his love for his parents; for great was the change that had taken place in his feelings since he had last been within its walls. After remaining some time engaged in devotion, his eyes were ever turning to where his parents and brothers sat, while theirs **as often** met his gaze; **still** they did not know him. At length his mother recognised him; and, forgetful of all but that she **saw** before her her long lost son, she uttered a cry of joy, and rushed towards him.

After remaining **at home for some** time, to enjoy the society **of his family and friends,** Alexander Selkirk **entered the Royal** Navy. He rose to **the rank of lieutenant,** and died on board H.M.S. *Weymouth* some time in **the** year 1723.

His sea-chest, his cocoa-nut shell **cup, and** other relics, were long preserved **and prized by his family** at Largo.

In the year **1741, the island of** Juan Fernandez was visited **by Lord Anson, who has** given **an account of the beauty of the** place, and the delights **of** the climate.

In the year 1814, the island was used as a state prison by the patriots of Chili, to which country it still belongs.

CHAPTER IV.

THE PAMPAS.

General Description—Storms in the Pampas—People—The Gauchos, or Indians of the Pampas—Other Indian Tribes—Terrible Adventure in the Pampas.

To the north of Patagonia and of the Rio Negro, between the Andes and the Atlantic Ocean, lie the immense plains of the Pampas, stretching away as far as the eye can reach, and surpassing in majesty and grandeur all the other wonders of the American continent. The inexpressible charm of these vast solitudes is the perfect freedom enjoyed there; but, on the other hand, they oppress and almost bewilder the mind from the air of sadness and monotony of which they everywhere bear the impress. In some places, one may travel two or three hundred miles without seeing the semblance of a rock or even a stone. On all sides there is excellent and nearly inexhaustible pasturage,—a carpet of high grass, diversified by the blossoms of the clover, or the colossal stems of the thistle, while here and there appear small lakes or lagoons, varying in size, and with no visible outlet. As the traveller approaches the Cordilleras,

PAMPAS GRASS.

the aspect of the country is somewhat changed. It becomes undulating, stony, and adorned with woods and forests, which grow thicker and finer as they extend towards the north.

There are few traces of life on the surface of the Pampas. Here and there, in a crack or crevice of the earth, the cactus hides its thorny head, or a solitary tree rises majestically upwards. Sometimes above you, you may observe a condor describing innumerable circles in the air, or perhaps you may see in the distance a *nandou* (a kind of ostrich, but with a more slender form), which seems to pass and disappear in a few moments, so rapid is its course.

The layer of *humus*, or good soil, on these plains varies in depth from one to three feet; under that there is a thick layer of clay, then a bed of sand. The ground is almost everywhere salt on the surface, and the waters brackish; but fresh, sweet water springs from the wells, which are dry to a certain depth.

Perhaps the most wonderful spectacles in the savannas of South America are the fierce storms which sweep over them. The *pampero* is in the Pampas what the *simoom* is in the great desert of Sahara. Masses of sand, raised by the storm, obscure the light of day, and even at noon thick darkness covers the earth. The roar of the thunder is mingled with the howling of the winds and the noise of the storm. Thousands of animals perish in the plain, and men lie prostrate with their faces on the ground till the tempest has passed by.

The population of this country is composed of whites of Spanish origin; gauchos, half white half Indian by birth; and Indians, still savage, and always much dreaded. The towns are chiefly inhabited by the whites; but many of them possess *estancias*, or farms, in the country, situated at a considerable distance from each other which must be

THE ESTANCIAS. 81

THE PAMPERO.

constantly provided with arms, and secured against the attacks of the Indians. The moderately rich among the proprietors have not less than fifty thousand head of cattle or horses. These have been astonishingly multiplied since the Spanish conquest, but they are half wild, and can only be taken when they are wanted by the help of a good horse and a lasso.

The true master of the Pampas is the gaucho—a half-savage shepherd, always on horseback. Covered with his *poncho*, a sort of cloak which clothes him from head to foot, still leaving his arms perfectly free—armed with the bola or with the lasso—his hunting-knife by his side—he casts over the plains a proud glance, expressive of his wild independence. This king of these solitudes fears only the Indian and the tiger; but the Indian is daily becoming more timid, and less to be feared; and as to the tiger, which ventures sometimes to approach the habitations of men, and to commit great ravages there, the gaucho dares boldly to wait for him, and meet him in the open country, and to struggle as it were in close combat with him. Watching the spring of the creature, and even his slightest movement—with his poncho rolled like a shield round his left arm, and his right armed with a cutlass—the gaucho bravely stabs the ferocious beast, and makes his skin into a saddle-cloth for his horse, or a mantle for his wife.

His own master from his childhood, the gaucho mounts a horse before he is four years old, and helps his parents to drive the cattle to their pasture-ground. When a little older, he spends his time in hunting, or tries to catch the wild horse of the plain, and subdue him. Indefatigable and restless, he often spends the night in the open air, with no covering but his cloak; hence his constitution is

LASSOING WILD HORSES.

inured to the greatest fatigue, and he becomes able to ride almost incredible distances. In consequence of such a life, the organs of his senses become acute to a most extraordinary degree. Every gaucho is a *rastreador*; that is to say, able to follow any creature by the trace of its steps. Amid these vast plains, where paths cross each other in all directions, and where the herds wander at will, he will distinguish the track of one animal among a thousand; he will know by the track of a horse whether he has been free or captive, whether loaded or not; and he will even tell the time when he has passed. If a theft has been committed under cover of night, and the rastreador be summoned in the morning, you may see him follow without hesitation the trace of footsteps across pathway and plain; cross or go up the bed of a stream; and in spite of all obstacles, reach at length the hiding-place of the guilty man, and say with perfect confidence, "Here is the thief!"

He passes his time in sleeping, gambling, hunting, gathering together the cattle from time to time to count or mark them, or killing and roasting the animals necessary for food. Such are his only occupations. He never eats bread, and the only kinds of fruits or vegetables known to him are the peach and the gourd. He lives entirely on animal food, and consumes about eight hundred pounds of meat in a year. He often roasts a whole animal entire on a long spit, and invites his friends to partake of it, when each guest cuts off for himself the piece he prefers. Water is their only drink. The hut of the gaucho is small and square, constructed of stakes wattled and interwoven with willows, covered with skins, and roofed with reeds or straw, a hole being left in the middle of the roof to let out the smoke.

The furniture and ornaments of his dwelling consist of stones for seats, a table, and sometimes a crucifix or an image of some saint (a memorial, perhaps, of his half-Spanish descent). Playing at cards is his greatest delight, and he will often spend whole days in gambling, seated on his heels, having always stuck in **the ground at** his side **his long** knife, from which **he** never separates, **ready** to pierce to the heart any one who should **dare** to cheat **or to provoke him.** For the lightest provocation, for **a** mere nothing, he hesitates not to draw out this long **knife** and stab his adversary. Then he mounts his horse and takes to flight, while all around him and on his way **warn** him of danger, and help him to escape from justice. When his horse falls down exhausted, he leaves it to the vultures, **and** catches a fresh one. When he is hungry, he dashes in among the herds of cattle, takes one **with the** lasso, **cuts** out a raw slice of its flesh, **and** lets the creature **go.** As a murderer and **a fugitive, he** is well received everywhere; **for** among **these** barbarous people, **where** neither religion **nor law** has any power—where the priests **are** as rude and wicked as their people—the public sympathy is always in favour of the guilty, and almost never on the side of the unfortunate victims of cruelty, **or** of the representatives of law and justice.

Several different nations of Indians, a wild and miserable race, are also scattered **over** the vast solitudes of the Pampas; the Puelches, or Indians of the East; the Huilliches, **or** Indians **of** the West; those near the Rio Negro, &c. These nations are subdivided into several hundreds of **tribes,** each ruled by a chief whom they choose, **and** who are called *caciques.* **They** neither build villages, houses, nor **even** huts; but inhabit portable tents, which they **make** by covering a frame of canes or reeds, with the skins of young horses, **whose flesh** they have devoured half raw. Horse flesh **is** their principal food, with the addition sometimes of a kind of bread or cake made of the meal of maize or wheat, which they buy from the Spaniards, giving them in exchange salt, cattle, and coverings of hair woven by their wives. They are wanderers, and will not take the trouble to cultivate the soil. Both men and women paint their faces with various bright colours, which adorns them exceedingly in their own eyes, and renders them most horrible in the eyes of strangers. They cover their shoulders with a sort of mantle, and tie round their waists a square piece of stuff, which they fasten by means of thongs of leather; several of them complete this dress by a conical hat, and a great pair of gaucho boots. The women delight in covering their fingers with rings of gold and silver, and suspending enormous earrings from their ears.

The love of plunder, drunkenness, and laziness, are the essential characteristics of the Indian of the Pampas. All the hard work to be done falls to the lot of his wife, who is, properly speaking, his slave. The Romanist missionaries who have gone among them, have never been able to do them the least good. They profess to believe in a Supreme Being, and in the immortality of the soul; but their religion chiefly consists in the practice of sorcery. They are formidable on account of the frequent *razzias*, or plundering expeditions, which they undertake to carry off the herds of their neighbours. Endowed with the most piercing sight, they keep a watch on all that passes in the plains of the Pampas, keeping themselves out of sight. When they think that they have a favourable opportunity, they dart like a cloud **of** vultures on the *estancias*, or farms—which are ill guarded—seize horses, **cattle,** and sometimes even women **and** children, whom they make their slaves, **and** after having stolen perhaps thousands **of** cattle, they go back to the **Andes to sell** their plunder; for the people of Chili, with **a** guilty indifference to right or justice, encourage **these robbers** by buying from them the **spoil** which they **know** perfectly well **to** have been stolen in the Pampas.

Such are the inhabitants, and such the general character of the country which **was** the scene **of** the following adventure:—

At an early hour **(says a traveller) I** crossed the threshold **of the farm where we** had been hospitably received **on our** journey. I longed **to** breathe the fresh morning air, and to bathe my feverish limbs in the cool stream; for I had been tormented all the night with the stings of innumerable insects. Putting my pistols in my belt and my rifle on my shoulder, I descended into a ravine, through which ran **one of** the numerous streams which flow **down from the Andes.**

Impatient to refresh myself **in the** clear, cool water, I did not pause to look **at the** beauty of the scene around me; but hastily undressing, I was proceeding to bathe, when all **at** once I heard **a** slight rustling among the shrubs and bushes which clothed the sides of **the** ravine. I was quite aware that I was in **a** dangerous situation. I knew that **the** Pampas were infested **by bands of** Indian savages, who had shortly before pillaged and desolated several villages situated at the foot of the

Andes. Soon I heard a cry of terror, and I immediately threw myself from the rock where I stood into the stream. I felt at the moment a sharp pain in my leg, and I perceived by the red colour of the water that I had been wounded. Looking up, I saw the dark form of an Indian warrior appearing through the bushes. He was almost naked, and his head was adorned with feathers. Before he had time to draw another arrow from his quiver, and bend his bow, I sprang out of the stream, seized my rifle, and, sheltering myself behind a rock, I levelled it at the Indian. He disappeared like lightning, and hid himself again among the bushes.

The cry of terror I had heard had been uttered by one of the servants belonging to the farm who, alarmed at seeing me go out so early, had followed me to the brink of the ravine. This cry had aroused all the inmates of the farm, as well as my travelling companions, who now came flocking round me. They beat the bushes, discovered the Indian warrior, who, struck by a rifle ball, rolled down to the bottom of the ravine, and was recognised as one of the chiefs of the Indian tribes who had laid waste the villages near the Andes. We soon after heard that several other Indians belonging to the same tribe had been seen prowling about in the neighbourhood of the farm. This news caused us some alarm, and we returned to the *hacienda*, to consult as to the measures necessary for safety during the rest of our journey.

Ten days before we had quitted San Jago, the capital of Chili, on our way to Buenos Ayres, the capital, or at least the chief city of the Confederation of Rio de la Plata. Our party consisted of four travellers, three guides, and four *rancheros* for servants. It was necessary for us to cross the Pampas, and guides are indispensable in a country where there are no roads; they are also useful in procuring fresh horses for travellers when their own are worn out. We had arrived the previous evening at the *hacienda* of San Jacintho, situated about thirty leagues on the eastern slope of the Andes. There we found a relay of guides; those who had brought us through the defiles and across the precipices of the mountains quitted us here, and a new set of guides undertook to conduct us across the Pampas, and were to leave us a few leagues from Buenos Ayres.

After having held a council, the majority were of opinion that the Indians who had alarmed us were only a small band of scouts detached from the main body of the tribe, and we resolved to continue our journey. One of our companions, however, quitted us, preferring to return to Chili with a numerous party of travellers, to exposing his life with us to the attacks of the Indians. I left the *hacienda*, therefore, with only two companions and our guides. By the advice of the latter, we descended into the ravine, and it was not till after we had followed the course of the stream for a distance of some leagues that we again ascended the bank, and entered the Pampas.

Having reached the plain, we put our horses to the gallop, and when two hours before sunset we stopped to rest, we calculated that we were already about twenty leagues distant from the *hacienda*. Our guides cut the grass round us to form a sufficient space for our encampment; they lighted a fire, and we took our evening meal. As a measure of precaution, instead of leaving our horses to graze at liberty, we tied them to stakes which our guides had brought with them.

Just as the sun was disappearing below the horizon, one of the *rancheros* uttered a cry of alarm, and drew our attention to a point in the distance, where we could just distinguish a troop of Indian horsemen rapidly advancing towards us by the way we had come.

It was a moment of deep anxiety; what should we do? Supposing that they were enemies, our horses were so wearied that flight was impossible; we resolved then to wait for the Indians, and to prepare for a contest. We saddled our horses, we gave arms to our servants, we loaded our rifles and our pistols. Meantime the Indians were fast coming nearer, they were about sixty in number; their wild cries resounded in our ears. They stopped at the distance of about two hundred paces from our little group. One of them came forward alone; he was armed with a bow, a hunting-knife, and a heavy tomahawk suspended from his shield; his companions were armed like himself; they had no firearms.

He advanced within the range of our rifles. We had still some hope that these Indians might not belong to the tribe whose chief had that morning fallen by our hands. One of our guides approached the Indian chief, and said a few words to him in the language of the **country; the two** others followed him and **also** spoke, but none of them received any reply. **The Indian** continued to gaze at us tranquilly. **At** length, **as if a** sudden thought had struck him, **he** turned quickly round and rejoined his troop. **At** his command the Indians **spread their ranks,** and keeping beyond the **range** of our guns, they formed a circle to surround us. The decisive moment was come; we mounted our horses and placed ourselves back to back, **so as** to face our enemies on all sides. **Assailed** by **a** shower of arrows, we replied **by a** discharge of musketry. One of my companions fell **dead** at my side. We put our horses **to the** gallop, and passed through the **ranks of our** enemies. Night was coming **on,** and we hoped to profit **by the** darkness to escape and return to the *hacienda.* I saw the knives of two Indians gleaming over my head. I knocked down one of them with a blow of my rifle. My horse, made furious by a wound, rushed wildly through my enemies, and carried me beyond the reach of their arrows. I heard their voices behind me in pursuit, apparently very near. My horse was staggering faint with loss of blood which was flowing fast from his wound. Hoping that, freed from my weight, he would run more easily, I dismounted, and lying down on the ground, I hid myself among the long grass. A moment after about twenty Indians **on** horseback passed on without perceiving me. When they were at some distance, I rose and began to make my way through the long grass, not without great difficulty. **A** short time after I again heard the gallop of the Indians' horses. I concluded that they had overtaken my horse, and finding him without a rider, that they had returned to seek me. I continued to walk on through the dry grass, when turning for a moment to look round, I perceived a reddish light.

The Indians had set fire to the grass, in order to cut off my retreat by surrounding me with a circle of fire. Numerous as they were, they might set fire to the plain without much risk to themselves, as they had been able with great ease to clear a sufficient space in which they would stand with safety, but a solitary man could have no hope of escape in this way. I resolved then to redouble my speed, in order to escape from the flames which pursued me, but I was soon forced to abandon this hope. The fire swept with such rapidity along the dry plains, that I saw myself condemned to perish in the flames. They lighted up the plain all around me, when, all at once, by the merciful guidance of Providence, I saw at a little distance the dead body of the horse which had shared my dangers. A bright idea flashed across my mind, and it seemed to me that this poor animal might furnish me with a means of escape. I took my hunting-knife, and cut away the grass all round me, so as to form a small circle within which the flames could not spread; but this circle was very small, and the near approach of the fire prevented me from enlarging it. Then I cut open my horse, I tore out the entrails, and sheltered myself within the still warm body.

No words can give any idea of the horror of this scene. On all sides, as far as I could see, there were masses of flame more than twenty feet in height

THE PAMPAS ON FIRE.

surmounted by clouds of black smoke. There was not a breath of air, and yet the fire swept along as rapidly as if it were driven before a tempest. The few minutes which elapsed before the flames had passed by the little circle within which I lay were a time of inexpressible anguish; the fire was around me, above me, within me; I seemed to breathe the fiery breath of a furnace. My blood was as if dried up, my brain seemed ready to burst—God alone could save me in this hour of fearful peril, and a fervent prayer arose to him from the very depths of my heart.

At length the danger lessened, my body was no longer within reach of the flames, but I had lost all consciousness. When I recovered from my faint, I was tormented by a burning thirst; I cut off a morsel of the flesh of my horse and sucked the blood. A little revived, I thought of the means of escape. The country was unknown to me, but I was certain that I could not fail to be taken if I returned in the direction of San Jacintho. I had heard the guide say that towards the south there were numerous ravines through which flowed the streams which came down from the mountains. I went in this direction as nearly as I could guess, with the hope of reaching one of these ravines before the dawn of day; but I could scarcely support myself. I threw down my gun and everything which I could do without, keeping only my pistols and a piece of the flesh of my horse.

After having walked for some hours over the plains blackened by the burning, I at length perceived a few bushes. I went towards them, and reached the brink of a ravine which formed the bed of a torrent. I easily quenched the thirst which tortured me, and I plunged into the **cool**, refreshing water dressed as I was. Towards the **end** of the day I began to feel hungry, for since the morning **I had** walked at least twelve leagues without food. Overwhelmed with fatigue and hunger, I **lay** down on the brink of **the** ravine, **and after having** given humble and hearty thanks to God for this first deliverance, I fell **into a** deep sleep. The coldness of the night **air** awoke me about an hour before sunrise; my limbs were stiffened, and I walked on in order **to** warm myself. I continued to walk **all the** morning under the fiery rays of a burning sun, till at length, exhausted with fatigue, **heat, and** hunger, **I lay** down on **the edge of the stream.**

After I had escaped the fire, **must I** then die of hunger? **I saw** neither birds nor animals of any kind that I could catch—my trust in God was beginning to fail, when I perceived **a** great water serpent which had come out of the stream, and was gliding away towards the clefts of the rock. **I broke** its back with **a** blow from a stone, and I finished it **with my** hunting-knife. I cut off its head, the only part which could be venomous, and gathering some brushwood and dry sticks, plentiful on the edge of the **ravine, I** lighted a fire and broiled the body of the serpent. Excessive hunger made me think this strange food delicious. Having thus restored a little my exhausted strength, **I** took with me the remains of the serpent which **I** had broiled whole, and continued my **journey. I passed a** whole day and night without any other **food** than the serpent's flesh. The further **I** advanced, the broader the ravine became, and I at length reached a place where it received another stream from the north. The burning of the plain had not extended beyond this, and I found myself again among the long grass of the Pampas.

On the fourth day I succeeded in killing a young buffalo, which, with several other animals of the same kind, had plunged into the water to get rid of the myriads of flies and mosquitoes which tormented him. The rest of the troop pursued me, and I only succeeded in escaping them by scrambling up a rock which they could not climb. A second pistol shot frightened them, and they disappeared in the plains. I cut off some slices of meat from the one I had killed, and broiled them. Strengthened by such a good repast, I proceeded on my way, taking with me a few slices of the broiled beef wrapped in one of the sleeves of my coat. I had been obliged to take off my coat and throw it away. It had been so saturated with the blood of the horse, that the heat had brought flies and worms upon it, and it was so disgusting that I could not keep it on. The rest of my dress was much in the same state, but I managed to wash it in the stream.

Through all my difficulties I did not lose courage. Full of confidence and faith in the merciful Providence who had preserved me so far, I continued my march, hoping soon to reach some hospitable shelter.

On the morning of the eighth day I had reached the foot of the first mountain ridge, and I was walking in a direction which I hoped might lead to some village, when I heard the sound of the bells of a troop of mules. A few minutes afterwards I found myself in the midst of a party of muleteers, who were carrying leather and tallow to the little town of San Juliana. I gave thanks from the very depths of my heart to God who had so graciously preserved me through so many dangers.

As I had some money with me, I easily managed to procure the few things that were absolutely necessary for the moment from the mule-drivers, and I agreed to accompany them to the place of their destination. There, by means of my letters of credit, I procured what money I needed, and set off again for the *hacienda* which I had left eight days before.

The Indians of the Pampas are indeed formidable foes, from whom it is difficult to escape. The occupation of their lives is war (says Sir Francis Head); they consider fighting as their noble and most natural employment; and they declare that the proudest attitude of the human figure is when, bending over his horse, man is riding at his enemy. The profession of the Indian is war; his food is simple; and his body is in that state of health and vigour that he can rise naked from the plain on which he has slept, and proudly look upon his image, which the white frost has marked out upon the grass, without inconvenience. Living in a boundless plain, all his occupations and amusements must necessarily be on horseback; and from being constantly accustomed to ride the Indians can scarcely walk. When they assemble to attack their enemies they collect large troops of horses, and uttering the wild shriek of war they start at a gallop. As soon as the horses they ride are tired, they vault upon the bare backs of fresh ones, keeping their best till they positively see their enemies. The whole country affords pasture for their horses; and whenever they choose to stop they have only to kill some mares for their repast. The ground is the bed on which, from their infancy, they have always slept; the flesh of mares, the food on which they have ever been accustomed to subsist, without either bread, fruit, or vegetables. They are, therefore, unencumbered by baggage or provision waggons. How impossible would it be for an European army to contend with such an aërial force! As well might it attempt to drive the swallows from the country as to harm these naked warriors.

CHAPTER V.

STATE OF LA PLATA, ETC.

La Plata—Republic of Paraguay—Uruguay—Buenos Ayres—Story of Maldonata.

THE region of the Pampas is of immense extent, and comprises a great number of different states. Most of these united in a vast confederation form the Argentine Republic or confederation of Rio de la Plata. The chief of these states, called by the name of their capital town, **are** those of Mendoza, **Cordova**, Santa Fé, Corrientes, &c. Near them, but more towards the north, is situated the republic of Paraguay; a country famous for its curious tea, which is made of the young leaves of a kind of holly known by the name of *maté*, used all over South America to make a drink like the tea of China. Assumption, the capital of this small state, is an unimportant town. Upon the frontiers of Brazil, to the east of the Argentine Confederation, is situated the small republic of Uruguay, whose capital, Monte Video, is a very commercial town, which attracts many foreign merchants, and exports to Europe an enormous quantity of raw hides and leather, of wool and tallow, of the bones and horns of cattle; the produce of the innumerable flocks and herds which graze on the Pampas.

The principal city of this country, which was long its capital and centre, and which, now separated from the confederation, forms a republic by itself, is the city of Buenos Ayres (literally, good air) a large town containing 100,000 inhabitants, which is becoming yearly more prosperous; and which we might suppose destined for a brilliant future, if in such a country there were any certain hope of a lasting peace on a solid foundation.

STORY OF MALDONATA:

A LEGEND OF BUENOS AYRES.

There have been great changes at Buenos Ayres since 1555, the year when the city was founded, amidst numerous tribes of hostile and warlike Indians. Many and terrible were the vicissitudes of the infant settlement; and an interesting legend is still preserved among the people, which may serve to give some idea, at least, of the trials and dangers to which the early colonists were exposed.

A short time after its first foundation, the new city was threatened by famine. All who attempted to go out in search of provisions were massacred by the savages, and it was found necessary to prohibit any one from leaving the enclosure of the walls on pain of death.

Yet a woman, to whom hunger had given courage to brave death, eluded the vigilance of the guards who had been placed round the colony. The fugitive was named Maldonata. After having wandered for some time in unknown and desert paths, she entered a cavern to rest. Imagine her terror when she saw a lioness in the cave, **and her** surprise when this formidable creature approached **her**, trembling, **and began to caress her** and lick her hands, uttering cries **of** pain more fitted to excite compassion than fear. The Spanish woman saw that the poor lioness **was** very ill; she **at once**, with great presence of mind, returned her caresses, brought her water to drink in the beaver hat which she wore, and tried to soothe and relieve the sufferings of **the** poor animal. Her cares were well repaid, the lioness recovered, and soon went **in search of food,** which she divided between her young **ones and** her kind attendant. Maldonata shared every day the food of the little lions, which played with her and amused her, while their mother provided for all. So time passed, till the young lions were old enough to go to seek their own food; the family of the cave then dispersed in the woods, and the lioness, **no** longer summoned home by the wants of her cubs, disappeared also, and **went** further into the desert in pursuit of her prey.

Maldonata, left alone and without any means **of** subsistence, was obliged also to leave the **cave,** where her gentle kindness to the sick lioness had made a temporary home. She wandered away, not knowing where she went, and she soon fell into the hands of Indian savages—more cruel than wild beasts. A lioness **had** cherished and fed her; but men made her a slave. Soon after she was retaken by **the** Spaniards, who led her back to Buenos

Ayres. The governor, more cruel than lions or savages, did not think her sufficiently punished by her sufferings, for her escape contrary to his edict. He sentenced her to be tied to a tree in the midst of the wood, there either to die of hunger, or to become the prey of wild beasts.

The cruel sentence was executed; and two days after, a party of soldiers were sent to see what had become of their victim. They found her alive, in the midst of hungry tigers, which were glaring at her with greedy eyes and open mouths; but which did not dare to approach her, because a fierce lioness and several young lions lay at her feet, as if to guard her from harm. At such a sight the soldiers stood motionless with terror and surprise. When the lioness perceived them, she slowly left the foot of the tree, as if to permit them to approach and unbind her benefactress; but after they had done this, the poor animal returned, and again crouched at Maldonata's feet, licking her hands. The grateful lioness continued to follow the woman to the very limit of the wood, showing in every possible way her regret at losing her.

The soldiers on their return reported to the governor all that had taken place; and the story of the humanity of a wild beast recalled to him, in some degree, the human feelings which he seemed to have left behind him when he crossed the sea from Europe to America. He permitted poor Maldonata to live, as she had been so miraculously preserved from death by a merciful Providence.

Meantime the Indian tribes, which were hovering round the Spanish colony, with the intention of blockading, and finally starving the people, drew their lines closer and closer round them. The only hope of the Spaniards appeared to be in a speedy return to Europe; but they had heard that there was gold to be found in the interior of the country, and the expectation of finding some of this ever-valued treasure encouraged them to endure, and nerved them to a desperate resistance. They quitted, however, the city of Buenos Ayres, and founded the town of Assumption, on the banks of the river, at three hundred leagues' distance from the sea. This seemed imprudent, as it was cutting themselves off from all help from the metropolis; but, in their eyes, it was bringing them nearer the treasures they so much coveted, and their avarice was still greater than their foresight.

The savage inhabitants of the country where they settled, proved to be either less courageous than the people of Buenos Ayres, or more easy to civilize. Far from disturbing the Spaniards at their work, they gladly supplied them with food. This conduct gave some hope that it might be possible for the Spaniards to attach them to themselves, and even to persuade them to learn their religion. In order to this, everything was done to allure them by ceremonies, not altogether unlike the heathen rites to which they had been accustomed. A procession took place on the great saints' days of the Popish Church, when all the colonists appeared with their shoulders bared, and carrying the instruments of flagellation in their hands. The Indians, who were invited to be present at this ceremony, so strange to them, went in a body, numbering eight thousand men, armed with bows and arrows, which they always wore, as they had vowed not to lay them down till they had drowned the invading strangers in their own blood.

The moment fixed for the massacre had come, and its execution seemed certain; when Irala, the Spanish commander, was warned by an Indian in his service of the existence of a conspiracy so little suspected till then.

Upon this the General caused a report to be circulated, that the settlement was in danger of being attacked by the savage Topiges.

He ordered his troops to arm themselves, and he summoned the chiefs of the savages, on pretence of taking counsel with them about the common danger. As soon as he had thus got the leaders of the conspiracy in his power, Irala put some of them to death, and threatened others with the same fate. The unfortunate men who survived, threw themselves at his feet, and obtained their pardon by swearing in their own name, and in the name of their nation, to yield implicit and unquestioning obedience to the Spaniards. This reconciliation, which seems to have been sincere on both sides, was sealed by the several marriages between the Spaniards and the Indians; and it is from the union of these races, so unlike each other, that the *metis*, or half-bloods are descended, now so numerous over all South America.

At a later period, the colonisation of Buenos Ayres was again resumed without difficulty; and this city has ever since continued to prosper.

CHAPTER VI.

THE EMPIRE OF BRAZIL.

General Description—Its vast Rivers—First Discovery and Subsequent History—Arrival of Don John VI. from Portugal—Brazil Declared a Kingdom—Don John Returns to Portugal—Revolution—Brazil Acknowledged Independent—Don Pedro I. Crowned Emperor—His Abdication—The Present Emperor Don Pedro II.

BRAZIL is the second country of the western world, and the leader of the South American States. It is thirty-five times the size of Great Britain, and occupies all the eastern part of South America. "It would seem as if Providence had designed this land as the residence of a great nation. Nature has heaped up her bounties of every description: cool breezes, lofty mountains, vast rivers, and plentiful rains, are treasures far surpassing the sparkling gems and the rich minerals which abound within the borders of this extended territory. No burning sirocco sweeps over this fair land to wither and desolate it; and no vast desert, as in Africa, separates its fertile provinces. That awful scourge, the earthquake, which causes strong men to become weak as infants, and which is constantly devastating the cities of Spanish America, disturbs no dweller in this empire. While in a large part of Mexico, and also on the west coast of South America—from Copiapo to the fifth degree of south latitude—rain has never been known to fall, Brazil is refreshed by copious showers, and is endowed with broad flowing rivers, cataracts, and sparkling streams. The Amazon, or, as the aborigines term it, *Pará*—"the father of waters"—with his mighty branches, irrigates a surface equal to two-thirds of Europe; and the San Francisco, the Parahiba do Sul, the vast affluents of the La Plata, under the names of the Paraguay, Parana, Cuiba, Paranahiba, and a hundred other streams of lesser note, moisten the fertile soil, and bear their tributes to the ocean through the southern and eastern portions of the empire. Let any one glance at the map of Brazil, and he will instantly be convinced that this land is designed by nature for the sustenance of millions.

Brazil is a land of rivers and streams, well watered and fertile; while in Peru, on the other side of the great continent, rain never falls, and the country is dry and comparatively barren. Mr. Fletcher says, "I have seen the western and eastern coasts of South America within thirty days of each other, and the former seemed a desert compared with the latter." What is the reason of this? Captain Maury thus answers the question. He says, "The coast of Peru is within the region of perpetual south-east trade winds. Though the Peruvian shores are on the verge of the great South Sea boiler, yet it never rains there. The reason is plain. The south-east trade winds in the Atlantic Ocean first strike the water on the coast of Africa. Travelling to the north-west, they blow obliquely across the ocean until they reach the **coast** of Brazil. By this time they are heavily laden with vapour, which they continue to bear along **across the** continent, depositing it as they go, and **supplying with it** the sources of the Rio de La Plata, **and the** southern tributaries of **the Amazon.** Finally, they reach the snow-capped **Andes,** and here is wrung from them the last particle **of** moisture that that very low temperature can extract. Reaching the summit of that range, they now tumble down **as cool and dry** winds on the Pacific slopes beyond. **Meeting** with no evaporating surface, **and with no** temperature *colder* than that to which they were subjected on the mountain-tops, they **reach the ocean** before they **become charged** with fresh vapour, and before, therefore, they have any which the Peruvian climate can extract. Thus we see how the top of the Andes becomes the reservoir from which are supplied the rivers of Chili and Peru."

Brazil was first discovered **by** Vincent Yanez Pinzon, who was a companion of Columbus, and commanded the *Nina* in that first glorious voyage which made known to the old world the existence of the new. He sailed again from Palos in December 1499; and crossing the equator, his eyes were gladdened by a green promontory, which he called Cape Consolation. This is now known as Cape St. Augustine, the headland just south of Pernambuco, one of the chief cities in Brazil. He sailed thence northward, and discovered **the** mouths of the Amazon and Orinoco. He took possession of this goodly land in the name of Castile; but before he reached

ITS CONQUEST BY PORTUGAL.

Spain, a Portuguese expedition, under the command of Pedro Alvarez Cabral, had also reached the Brazilian coast, and claimed it for Portugal. He named it Vera Cruz (the true cross), and set up a large cross as the memorial of his visit. The Pope of Rome, who, in those days, pretended to the power of giving away countries he had never seen, according to his own good pleasure, decided the disputed claim, and the Portuguese became masters of Brazil. Don Emanuel, king of Portugal, sent out another expedition to his new dominions; and in one of the vessels sent was Americus Vespucius, the Florentine, whose name has been given to the whole great continent. He was also the means of changing the name of Brazil, which Cabral had named Vera Cruz. The most valuable part of the cargo which Americus Vespucius carried back to Europe, on his second expedition to Brazil, was the well-known dye-wood, *Cæsalpinia Braziliensis*,—called, in the Portuguese language, *pan brazil*, on account of its resemblance to *brazas*, "coals of fire;" the land whence it came was termed the "Land of the Brazil Wood;" and finally this appellation was shortened to Brazil, and completely usurped the names *Vera Cruz*, or *Santa Cruz*.

Brazil was governed by viceroys from Portugal till the year 1807, when that kingdom was involved in the troubles of the European continent. Threatened by Napoleon, the vacillating Prince Regent of Portugal, Don John VI., was induced, after much hesitation, to declare war against England,—too late to pacify the French emperor. An English fleet, under Sir Sidney Smith, appeared at the mouth of the Tagus; and the British ambassador left no other alternative to Don John VI., than to surrender to England the Portuguese fleet, or to avail himself of the British squadron for the protection and transportation of the royal family to Brazil. The moment was critical, for the army of Napoleon had penetrated the mountains of Beira. No resource remained to the Prince Regent but to choose between a tottering throne in Europe, and a vast empire in America. There was no time for indecision. The archives, treasures, and most precious effects of the crown were transferred to the Portuguese and English fleets; and on the 29th of November 1807, accompanied by his family and a multitude of faithful followers, the Prince Regent took his departure amid the combined salvos of the cannon of Great Britain and of Portugal. That very day Marshal Junot thundered upon the heights of Lisbon, and the next morning took possession of the city.

The fugitive royal family were welcomed in Brazil with every possible manifestation of joy. The city of Rio de Janeiro was illuminated for nine successive evenings.

From that time may be dated many improvements in Brazil; the whole face of the country underwent great and rapid changes. Before this time all commerce and intercourse with foreigners had been rigidly prohibited by the narrow policy of Portugal. The printing press had not made its appearance, books and learning were rare, the people were in every way made to feel their dependence, and the spirit of industry and enterprise were alike unknown.

The first act of the Prince Regent was to give that *carta regia*, which opened the ports of Brazil to the commerce of the world. A printing press was introduced, and a Royal Gazette was published. Academies of medicine and the fine arts were established. The Royal Library, containing sixty thousand volumes of books, was opened for the free use of the public. Foreigners were invited, and embassies from England and France took up their residence at Rio de Janeiro. Foreign commercial houses were opened, and foreign artizans established themselves in Rio and other cities.

This country could no longer remain a colony. A decree was promulgated in 1815, declaring it elevated to the dignity of a kingdom, and hereafter to form an integral part of the United Kingdom of Portugal, Algarves, and Brazil. Soon after this the Queen Donna Maria I. (who had long been imbecile) died, and her son, the Prince Regent, was crowned King in 1818.

Tranquillity followed the erection of Brazil into a constituent portion of the kingdom, but it was of short duration. Discontent was at work. There were jealousies between the newly-arrived Portuguese and the native Brazilians. The revolution which occurred at Portugal in 1821 in favour of a constitution, was immediately responded to by a similar one in Brazil. After much excitement and alarm from the tumultuous movements of the people, the King Don John VI. conferred upon his son Don Pedro, Prince Royal, the office of regent and lieutenant to his majesty in the kingdom of Brazil. He then hastened his departure for Portugal, accompanied by the remainder of his family, and the principal nobility, who had followed him. He embarked on board a line of battle-ship on the 24th of April 1821. Just as the vessel was ready to sail, the old king pressed his son to his bosom for the last time, and exclaimed: " Pedro, Brazil will, I fear, ere long separate herself from Portugal, and if so, place the crown on thine own head rather than allow it to fall into the hands of any adventurer."

The old king's prediction was soon realized. The prince had left Portugal so young that his sympathies and feelings were associated with the land of his adoption. He found himself surrounded with difficulties. The Cortes of Portugal, jealous of his position, ordered him to return to Europe. The Brazilians entreated him to remain with them, and urged him to declare the country independent, and assume the title of emperor. He at first refused, but the measures of the Cortes of Portugal continued to be arbitrary in the extreme towards Brazil; and at length, while the prince was on a journey to the province of San Paulo, he received despatches from the mother country, which had the effect of putting an end to all hesitation and delay. On the 7th of September 1822, when he read these despatches, he was surrounded by his courtiers, on the beautiful campinas in sight of San Paulo,—a city which had ever been, as it is now, celebrated in Brazil for the liberality and intelligence of its inhabitants. It was then, on the margin of an insignificant stream, the Ypiranga, that he made that exclamation, " *Independencia ou morte!*" (Independence or death) which became the watchword of the Brazilian revolution; and from the 7th of September 1822, the independence of the country has since held its official date. It has been truly said that, in the eyes of the civilized world, it was a memorable circumstance, and must ever form an epoch in the history of the Western continent. It was indeed a great event, and led to vast results.

The Brazilian revolution was comparatively a bloodless one. The glory of Portugal was already waning, her resources were exhausted, and her energies crippled by internal dissensions. The Portuguese forces were soon compelled to withdraw, and leave Brazil to her own control. In less than three years from the time independence was declared on the plains of the Ypiranga, Brazil was acknowledged to be independent at the court of Lisbon. In the meantime, Don Pedro I. had been crowned emperor, and an assembly of delegates from the provinces had been convoked for the formation of a constitution. A liberal constitution was afterwards framed, and was accepted by the emperor in 1824. By this Brazil is still governed.

Jealousies, however, continued between the various parties in the state, and after a troubled rule of ten years, the emperor abdicated in favour of his son, Don Pedro II., and returned to Europe in 1831, accompanied by his empress and his eldest daughter, Donna Maria, the late queen of Portugal.

With all his faults, Don Pedro was a great man; and as time rolls on, his merits are more recognised by the Brazilians. They have erected statues and public monuments to his memory, and entitle him, "*O Washington do Brazil.*"

The present emperor, Don **Pedro II., is a** learned and most accomplished prince. **It** has been **remarked that a stranger** can scarcely start a subject **in regard to his own** country that would be foreign **to the** emperor. **He is** acquainted, so far as **translating** is concerned, with every principal European tongue, and can converse in six languages. He is an enthusiastic chemist, and a good topographical engineer, and an artist. There **is** not **a** session of the Brazilian Historical Association from which **he is** absent, **and** he has been named **an** honorary **member of the New York** Historical Society. He is familiar with the modern literature **of** England, Germany, and the United States to a degree of minuteness absolutely surprising.

In stature he is indeed a Saul—head and shoulders above his people; and in his court dress, with his crown upon his fine fair brow, and his sceptre in his hand, whether receiving the salutes of his subjects, or opening the Imperial Chambers, he is a splendid specimen of manhood. His height, when uncovered, **is** 6 feet 4 inches, and his head and body are beautifully proportioned. At a glance one can see in that full brain and in that fine blue eye that he is not a mere puppet **upon** the throne, but a man who *thinks.* Under his constitutional rule, civil liberty, religious toleration, and general prosperity **are** better secured than in any other government of the New World, save where the Anglo-Saxon bears sway. In **1850,** the slave trade (which had continued despite solemn treaties) was effectually put down, and soon after a number of the leading dealers in the inhuman traffic — men who had hitherto held a high position in society—were banished. In Brazil, everything is in favour of freedom; and such are the facilities for the slave to emancipate himself, that it is probable slavery will be abolished altogether before another half century rolls round. By the Brazilian laws, a slave can go before a magistrate, have his price fixed, and purchase himself; and a man of mental endowments, even if he had been a slave, would be debarred from no official station, however high, unless it might be that of Imperial Senator. In the colleges, the medical, law, and theological schools, there is no distinction of colour.

In 1850, the first steamship line to Europe was established, and now the empire is united to the Old World by no less than eight lines. England's commerce with Brazil, since the establishment of her first steam line in 1850, has increased her exports more than 100 per cent. In 1856 alone, Great Britain imported from Brazil 21,830,000 pounds of cotton. The imports of coffee from Brazil to Britain were 3,000,000 pounds in 1852, and rose to 52,000,000 in 1853, 59,000,000 in 1854, and 112,000,000 in 1855. Brazil receives from Great Britain 54 per cent. of all her imports.

For the last ten years the progress of Brazil has been onward. Her public credit is of the highest character. Internal improvements have been projected, and are being executed, and tranquillity has prevailed. Why must we add that there is a dark

INFLUENCE OF POPERY.

side to the picture? Popery, with its accompanying ignorance, is still hanging like a drag on Brazil, keeping the masses sunk in darkness and superstition, and preventing the more rapid advance of this great nation. Yet even in this point of view there is hope. Although Popery is the established religion, it is not allowed to rule, and to this may be attributed the advance of Brazil beyond Mexico or the other South American States.*

---

* In addition to the foregoing sketch, we may remind the reader that for the last two years Brazil, in conjunction with the Argentine Republic, has waged war against Paraguay and its Dictator, Lopez, who has been driven out of all his strongholds.

CHAPTER VII.

RIO DE JANEIRO.

First Discovery of the Bay—Origin of the Name—The Beauty of the Scenery—The Sugar-Loaf—The Organ Mountains—Commercial Importance of Rio de Janeiro—Its Fine Harbour—General Aspect of the City.

WHAT a glorious spectacle must have presented itself to those early navigators—De Solis, Majellan, and Martin Affonso de Souza—who were the first Europeans that ever sailed through the narrow portal which constitutes the entrance to Nitherohy (Hidden Water), as these almost land-locked waters were appropriately and poetically termed by the Tamoya Indians! Though the mountain sides and borders of the bay are still richly and luxuriantly clothed, then all the primeval forests existed, and gave a wilder and more striking beauty to a scene so enchanting in a natural point of view, even after three centuries of the encroachments of man. De Souza, as the common tradition runs, supposed that he had entered the mouth of a mighty river, rivalling the Orinoco and the Amazon, and named it Rio de Janeiro (River of January), after the happy month—January 1531—in which he made his imagined discovery. Whatever may have been the origin of this misnomer, it is not only applied to the large and commodious bay, but to the province in which it is situated, and to the populous metropolis of Brazil, which sits like a queen upon its bright shores.

The first entrance of any one into the Bay of Rio de Janeiro forms an era in his existence. Even the dullest observer must afterwards cherish sublime views of the manifold beauty and majesty of the works of the Creator. I have seen the most rude and ignorant Russian sailor, the immoral and unreflecting Australian adventurer, as well as the cultivated and refined European gentleman, stand silent upon the deck, naturally admiring the gigantic avenue of mountains and palm-covered isles, which, like the granite pillars before the temple of Luxor, form a fitting colonnade to the portal of the finest bay in the world.

On either side of that contracted entrance, as far as the eye can reach, stretch away the mountains, whose pointed and fantastic shapes recall the glories of Alpland. On our left the Sugar-Loaf stands like a giant sentinel to the metropolis of Brazil. The round and green summits of the Tres Irmãos (Three Brothers) are in strong contrast with the peaks of Corcovado and Tijuca; while the Gavia rears its huge sail-like form, and half hides the fading line of mountains which extends to the very borders of Rio Grande de Sul. On the right another lofty range commences near the principal fortress, which commands the entrance of the bay, and, forming curtain-like ramparts, reaches away in picturesque headlands to the bold promontory

118   CAPE FRIO.

THE ORGAN MOUNTAINS.

well known to all South Atlantic navigators as
Cape Frio. Far through the opening of the bay,
and in some places towering even above the lofty
coast-barrier, can be discovered the blue outline of

the distant Organ mountains, whose **lofty** pinnacles **will at** once suggest the origin of their **name.**

As far up the bay as the **eye can reach, lovely,** little, verdant, and palm-clad islands **are to be** seen rising out of its dark **bosom;** while **the** hills and lofty mountains which surround **it on all** sides, when gilded by the rays of the setting sun, form **a** befitting frame for such a picture. At night the lights of **the** city have a fine effect; and when the land-breeze began to blow, the rich odour of the orange and other perfumed flowers **is** borne seaward along with it.

The city of Rio de Janeiro, or San Sebastian, **is at** once the commercial emporium **and the** political **capital of** the nation. While **Brazil** embraces **a** greater territorial dominion than **any** other country of the New World, together with natural advantages second to none on the globe, the position, the scenery, and the increasing magnitude of its capital, render it a metropolis worthy of the empire. Rio de Janeiro is the largest **city** of South America, the **third** in size on the western continent, and boasts an antiquity greater than that **of any** city in the United States.

Its harbour is situated just within the borders of the southern torrid zone, and communicates, **as** before described, with the wide-rolling Atlantic **by a** deep and narrow passage between two granite mountains. This entrance is so safe as to render **the** services **of a** pilot entirely unnecessary. So commanding, however, is the position of the various **fortresses at** the mouth **of** the harbour, upon its islands, and **on** the surrounding heights, that, if sufficiently manned by a **body** of determined men, they might defy the hostile ingress of the proudest navies in the world.

Once within this magnificent bay of Nitherohy, the wanderer of the seas may safely moor his bark within hearing of the roar of the ocean surf.

The aspect which Rio de Janeiro presents to the beholder bears no resemblance to the compact brick walls, the dingy roofs, the tall chimneys, and the generally even sites of our northern cities. Its surface is diversified by hills of irregular, but picturesque shape, which shoot up in different directions, leaving between them flat intervals of greater or less extent. Along the bases of these piles, and up their sides, stand rows of buildings, whose whitened walls and red-tiled roofs are in happy contrast with the deep green foliage that always surrounds, and often embowers them. The most prominent eminence, almost in front of us, is the Morro de Castello, which overlooks the mouth of the harbour, and on which is the tall signal-staff which announces, in common with the telegraph on Babylonia Hill, the nation, class, and position of every vessel that appears in the offing. Upon our right we see the convent-crowned hill of San Bueto; and if we could have a bird's-eye view from a point midway between the turrets of the convent and the signal-staff of Morro de Castello, we should see the city spread beneath us, with its streets, steeples, and towers, its public edifices, parks, and vermillion chimneyless roofs, and its aqueducts spanning the spaces between the seven green hills,—constituting a gigantic mosaic, bordered upon one side by the mountains, and on the other by the blue waters of the bay.

RIO DE JANEIRO.

From the central portion of the city the suburbs extend about four miles in each of the three principal directions; so that the municipality of Rio de Janeiro, containing 300,000 inhabitants, covers a greater extent of ground than any European city of the same population.

Here dwell a large part of the nobility of the nation; and for a considerable portion of the year the representatives of the different provinces, the ministers of state, the foreign ambassadors and consuls, and a commingled populace of native Brazilians and of foreigners from almost every clime. That which, in the popular estimation, however, confers the greatest distinction upon Rio, is not the busy throng of foreign and home merchants, sea captains, ordinary government officials, and the upper classes of society; but it is in the fact that here resides the imperial head of Brazil, the young and gifted Don Pedro II., who unites the blood of the Braganzas and the Hapsburgs, and under whose constitutional rule, civil liberty, religious toleration, and general prosperity, are better secured than in any other government of the New World, save where the Anglo-Saxon bears sway.

Rio de Janeiro will ever be memorable as the first spot in the Western Hemisphere where the banner of the reformed religion was unfurled. A Frenchman, named Nicholas Durand de Villegagnon, a knight of Malta, aspired to the honour of establishing a colony in the New World. He was an officer of distinction in the French service, and had been appointed to the honourable post of commander of the vessel which bore Mary, Queen of Scots, from France to her own country. He pretended to be a Protestant, and had the cunning and address to secure the patronage of the great and good Admiral Coligny, whose persevering attempt to plant the reformed religion in both North and South America was a leading feature in his life up to the time when St. Bartholomew's Eve was written in characters of blood.

Villegagnon proposed to found an asylum for the persecuted Huguenots. Admiral Coligny's influence secured to him a respectable number of colonists. The French Court was disposed to view with no small satisfaction the plan of founding a colony after the example of the Portuguese and Spanish. In 1555 Henry II. of France furnished three small vessels, of which Villegagnon took the command, and sailed from Havre de Grace. After a long and perilous voyage, he entered the Bay of Nitherohy and commenced fortifying a small island near the entrance, now denominated Lage, and occupied by a fort. His fortress, however, being of wood, could not resist the action of the water at flood-tide, and he was obliged to remove further upward, to the island now called Villegagnon, where he built a fort, at first named in honour of his patron Coligny. This expedition was well planned, and the place for a colony fitly chosen. The French were welcomed by the natives, who disliked the Portuguese.

It was upon this island that they erected their rude plan of worship, and here these French Puritans offered their prayers and sang their hymns of praise nearly threescore years and ten before a pilgrim placed his foot on Plymouth Rock, and more than half a century before the Book of Common Prayer was borne to the banks of the James River.

Many colonists from Europe were disposed to join this honourable bond of pioneers. The Church of Geneva became interested in the object, and ministers and students were appointed to go to the new colony. Had their leader been true, a noble and free State might soon have arisen in South America. But Villegagnon was a traitor—a Papist in disguise. As soon as he dared, he avowed his real opinions, and began to persecute the truth. Those who had come to the other side of the globe to enjoy liberty of conscience, found persecution where they had hoped for freedom. Many of them returned, and on their homeward voyage, ill provided with stores, they were reduced to the greatest misery. For want of food they not only devoured all the leather, even to the covering of their trunks, but in their despair they attempted to chew the hard, dry Brazil wood which happened to be in the vessel. Several died of hunger. They arrived in Europe just in time to undeceive a body of Flemish adventurers ready to embark for Brazil, and also about 10,000 Frenchmen who would have emigrated, if the object of Coligny in founding his colony had not been thus wickedly betrayed. Had it not been for the treachery of Villegagnon to the party to which he pretended to belong, Rio de Janeiro would probably have been at this day the capital of a French Protestant colony or of an independent State, free from the curse of Popery.

But those who would have joined the infant

colony having been deterred, by finding **that the** leader was **a traitor, the** small band who first went out were left to fight the battle alone. **The** French Court **was too** busy burning and massacring the Huguenots (as they called the Protestants) to think **of** Brazil; and Coligny, after his generous plans had been ruined **by the** treachery of Villegagnon, **no** longer **regarded the colony.** The day for emigration **from his** country was over; and they who should have colonized Rio de Janeiro were bearing arms against a bloody and implacable enemy in defence of everything dear to man.

On the 20th of January **1567 (called by the** Papists St. **Sebastian's day), the stronghold of the** French **was stormed by the** Portuguese, **who had settled on the mainland. All who loved** the truth **were** either murdered **or forced to fly.** The Portuguese governor traced out the plan of a new city, which he called **St.** Sebastian, after **the** idol of the day. He celebrated his victory by the death of the martyrs of the **truth; and thus** the new city was founded **in** blood. **The** name of St. Sebastian has been since changed **to Rio de** Janeiro, the name of **the** bay.

The author of "Brazil and La Plata" makes **the** following remarks in regard **to** the treachery **of** Villegagnon, and the consequent defeat of the first French colonists:—

"**With the** remembrance **of** this failure **in** establishing **the** reformed religion here, **and of** the direct cause which **led to it,** I often **found** myself speculating **as to** the possible **and** probable results which **would have followed** the successful establishment of

Protestantism during the three hundred years that have since intervened. With the wealth, power, and increasing prosperity of the United States before us, as the fruits, at the end of two hundred years, of the colonization of a feeble band of Protestants on the comparative bleak and barren shore of the northern continent, there is no presumption in the belief that, had a people of similar faith, similar morals, similar habits of industry and enterprise, gained an abiding footing in so genial a climate, and on a soil so exuberant, long ago the still unexplored and impenetrable wilderness of the interior would have bloomed and blossomed in civilization as the rose, and Brazil, from the sea-coast to the Andes, would have become one of the gardens of the world. But the germ which might have led to this was crushed by the bad faith and malice of Villegagnon; and, as I look on the spot which bears his name and perpetuates his reproach, the two or three solitary palms which lift their tufted heads above the embattled walls, and furnish the only evidence of vegetation on the island, seem, instead of plumed warriors in the midst of their defences, like sentinels of grief mourning the blighted hopes of the long past."

But we should not look too "mournfully into the past;" for though, in the mysterious dealings of Providence, no Protestant nation, with its attendant vigour and progress, sways it over that fertile and salubrious land, may we not, to a certain extent, legitimately consider the tolerant and fit constitution of the empire and its good government, the general material prosperity, and the advancement of the Brazilians, in every point of view, far beyond all other South American nations, as an answer to the faithful prayers with which those pious Huguenots baptized Brazil more than three centuries ago?

Yes! there is hope for Brazil. Popery, though established, is despised by all the intelligent natives of the country. It is there seen undisguised, as it really is,—a mixture of heathen rites and Christianity, idolatry with a Christian name, the worship of idols under the name of saints,—uncovered with the cloak of dissimulation which wily priests find it advisable to throw over it in our land of truth and light.

For example, in Bahia, a city of Brazil, they worship an image which they call St. Anthony, which was cast on shore by the waves, and which the people—poor ignorant Romanists—fancied had come direct either from heaven or from Rome (had they ever been in Italy they would have known that Rome and heaven are far apart). Protestants say that this was the figure-head of a wrecked ship, cast on shore by the currents which Lieutenant Maury has so well described. But Romanists in Brazil worship it; it was first promoted to the rank of captain, and then the bills for its washing, clothing, &c., are regularly paid by the deluded people to the Franciscan monks.

It may easily be believed that all intelligent men despise the Romanist Church, both for the ignorance and the immorality of the priests. They see that Romanism is falsehood, but they know not where to find the truth. An interesting remark was made by a Brazilian to an American missionary, who asked him what report he should give to the religious world respecting Brazil? "Say that we are in darkness, behind the age, and almost abandoned." "But that you wish for light?" "We wish for nothing. We are hoping in God, the Father of lights."

They are, at least, ready to receive the light. They are thankful for the Bibles distributed among them by the agents of the American Missionary and Bible Societies. The more the priests oppose the Bible, the more the people welcome it,—ready to cast off the yoke of falsehood. They appear willing to receive the joyful tidings of the gospel of Christ. May the light of truth in all its brightness yet beam on Brazil!

CHAPTER VIII.

VEGETABLE PRODUCTIONS OF BRAZIL.

Extent of Brazil—Its Vast Resources—Its **Productions, Mineral and Vegetable**—The Mandioc Root—Its Use **by the Natives—By the Portuguese**—Modes of Preparing it—Drink **made from it—The Palm Tree—Its Uses**—The Caoutchouc **or Gum-Elastic Tree—The Milk Tree**, &c.

BRAZIL has neither been explored nor surveyed, and its full extent cannot be accurately ascertained; but according to the best calculations made in 1845 for the "Diccionario Geographico Braziliero," the empire contains within its borders 3,004,460 square miles. The United States, by the latest computations of the Topographical Bureau at Washington, has an area of 2,936,166 square miles. Brazil is therefore 68,294 square miles larger than the whole territory of the Union; in other words, we should have to add to the possessions of the United States an area equal to that of the adjacent States of New York, Connecticut, Massachusetts, and Vermont, to make it of the same dimensions as the land of the Southern Cross. European Russia possesses an area of 2,142,504 square miles, and the remainder of Europe 1,687,626. It is by these figures and comparisons that we may arrive at an approximate idea of the vastness of Brazil.

It has already been seen that the internal resources of this empire are commensurate with its favoured position and its wide extent. It is neither the gold of its mines nor the diamonds that sparkle in the beds of its inland rivers that constitute the greatest sources of its available wealth. Although nature has bestowed upon Brazil the most precious minerals, yet she has been still more prodigal in the gift of vegetable riches. Embracing nearly five degrees north of the equator, the whole latitude of the southern torrid and ten degrees of the southern temperate zones, and stretching its longitude from Cape St. Augustine (the easternmost point of the continent) across the mountains of its own interior to the very foot of the Andes, its soil and its climate offer an asylum to almost every valuable plant. In addition to numberless varieties of indigenous growth, there is scarcely a production of either India which might not be naturalized in great perfection under or near the equator; while its interior uplands, and its soil in the far south, welcome many of the fruits, the grains, and the hardier vegetables of Europe.

It would take volumes, instead of a few pages, to describe all the rich and varied productions of Brazil,—coffee, cotton, and sugar are the chief. Its giant forests furnish inexhaustible supplies of fine wood, and its plains feed vast herds of cattle. Wheat and rice grow in some parts, but the mandioca is the principal farinaceous production of Brazil, and is as much associated with the sustentation of life in Brazil as wheat in more northern climes.

This vegetable (*Manihot utilissima*) is deserving of particular notice. Its **peculiarity is** the union of a deadly poison with highly nutritious qualities. It is indigenous **to** Brazil, and **was** known to the Indians long before the discovery **of** the country. **The little** cultivation to which **the** natives attended **was that** of this root, which, when planted **in burned** ground, thrives among the stumps **and** roots **of trees** without further husbandry. It **is** difficult to imagine how savages should have even discovered that a wholesome food might be prepared from this root.

Their mode of preparation was by scraping it **to** a **fine** pulp with oyster-shells, **or with an instrument** made **of small sharp** stones **set in a** piece **of bark, so as to** form a rude rasp. The pulp **was** then rubbed or **ground** with **a** stone, the juice carefully expressed, and the last remaining moisture evaporated by the fire. The operation of preparing it was thought unwholesome, and the slaves, whose business it was, took the flowers of the nhambi and the root **of the** urucu in their food, " **to** strengthen the **heart** and the stomach."

The Portuguese soon invented mills and presses for this purpose. They usually pressed it in cellars, and places where it was least likely to occasion accidental harm. In these places it is said that a white insect was found generated by this deadly juice, itself not less deadly, with which the native women sometimes poisoned their husbands, and slaves their masters, by putting it in their food. A poultice of mandioc, with its own juice, was considered excellent for imposthumes. It was administered for worms, and was applied to old wounds to eat away the diseased flesh. For some poisons also, and for the bite of certain snakes, it was esteemed a sovereign remedy. The simple juice was used for cleaning iron. The poisonous quality is confined to the root, for the leaves of the plant are eaten, and even the juice might be made innocent by boiling, and be fermented into vinegar, or inspissated till it became sweet enough to serve for honey.

The crude root cannot be preserved three days by any possible care, and the slightest moisture spoils the flour. Piso observes that he had seen great ravages occasioned among the troops by eating it in this state. There were two modes of preparation by which it could more easily be kept. The roots were sliced under water, and then hardened before a fire. When wanted for use, they were grated into a fine powder, which, being beaten up with water, became like a cream of almonds. The other method was to macerate the root in water, till it became putrid, then hang it up to be smoke-dried; and this, when pounded in a mortar, produced a flour as white as meal. It was frequently prepared in this manner by savages. The most delicate preparation was by pressing it through a sieve, and putting the pulp immediately in an earthen vessel on the fire. It then granulated, and was excellent when either hot or cold.

The native mode of cultivating it was rude and summary. The Indians cut down the forest trees, let them lie till they were dry enough to burn, and then planted the mandioc between the stumps. They ate the dry flour in a manner that baffled all imitation. Taking it between their fingers, **they** tossed it into their mouths so neatly that not **a** grain **was** lost. No European ever tried **to** perform this feat without powdering his face or his clothes, **to the** amusement of the **savages.**

The manioc **supplied them** also with **the** banqueting-drink. **They** prepared **it by an** ingenious process, **which savage** man **has** often been cunning enough **to invent,** but never cleanly enough to reject. The roots were sliced, boiled till they became soft, and set aside to cool. The young **women** then chewed them, after which they were returned into the vessel, which was filled with water, and **once** more boiled, being stirred **the whole** time. **When** this **process** had **been** continued sufficiently **long,** the unstrained contents were poured into earthen jars of great size, **and** buried **up** to the middle in the floor of the house. The jars were closely stopped, and in the course of two or three days fermentation took place. They had an old superstition that if it were made by men it would be good for nothing. When the drinking-day arrived, the women kindled **fires** around these jars, and served out the warm potion in half-gourds, which the men came dancing and singing to receive, and always emptied at one draught. They never ate at these parties, but continued drinking as long as one drop of liquor remained; and having exhausted **all** in one house, removed to the next, till they had drunk out **all in** the town. These meetings were commonly held once in **the** month. De Levy witnessed one which lasted **three days** and three **nights.** Thus man in **every** age **and** country gives proof of his depravity, by converting the gifts of a bountiful Providence into the means of his own destruction.

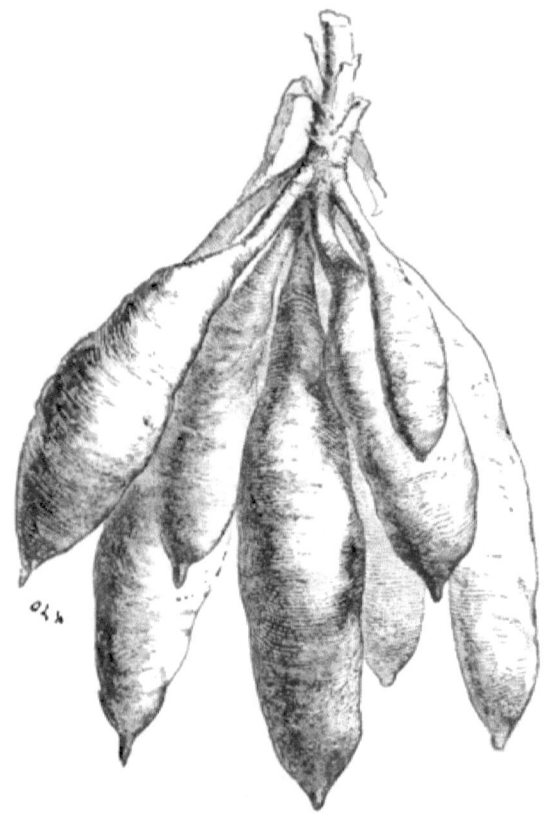

ROOTS OF MANIHOT OR MANDIOCA.

Mandioca is of slow growth, the more common species requiring from twelve to eighteen months to ripen. Its roots have a great tendency to spread. Cut slips of the plant are inserted in large holes, which at the same time counteract this tendency, and furnish it with a dry soil, which the mandioca prefers. The roots, when dry, are of a fibrous texture, corresponding in appearance to those of the long parsnip. **The** process of preparation is, first to boil them, then to remove the rind; after which **the** pieces **are** held **by** the hand in contact with a circular grater, turned by water-power. The pulverized material is **then** placed **in** sacks, several of **which, thus** filled, **are** subjected **to the action** of a screw-press for the expulsion of **the** poisonous liquid. The masses thus solidified **by** pressure are beaten fine in mortars. The substance is next transferred to open ovens, or concave plates, heated beneath, where it **is** constantly and rapidly stirred until quite dry. **The** appearance of the farina, when well prepared, is very **white and** beautiful, although its particles **are** rather **coarse.** It is found **upon every** Brazilian **table, and** forms **a** great variety **of** healthy and palatable dishes. **The** fine substance deposited by the juice **of the** mandioca, when preserved, standing a short time, constitutes the *tapioca* of commerce, so well known in the culinary departments of North America and Europe, and is now a valuable export from Brazil.

But the most generous gift of Providence to Brazil is the palm-tree. **The** traveller in the interior provinces and upon the sea-coast, away from the cities, **is** struck by the very great application **of this** "prince of the vegetable kingdom" **to the** wants of man. And if the prince plays so important a part in the domestic economy of Europeans and their descendants, his highness was, and is, servant for general house and field work among the aborigines of Brazil. To this day it furnishes the Amazonian Indians house, raiment, food, drink, salt, fishing-tackle, hunting implements, and musical instruments, and almost every necessary of life, except flesh. Take the hut of a Uaupé Indian, on one of the affluents of the Rio Negro. The rafters are formed by the straight and uniform palm called *Leopoldina pulchra*, the roof is composed of the Caraná palm, and the doors and frame-work of the split stems of the *Iriartea exporiza*. The wide bark which grows beneath the fruit of another species is sometimes used as an apron. The Indian's hammock, his bow-strings, and his fishing-lines are woven and twisted from the fibrous portions of different palms. The comb with which the males of some of the tribes adorn their heads is made from the hard wood of a palm, and the fish-hooks are made from the spine of the same tree. The Indian makes, from the fibrous spathes of the *Manicaria saccifera*, caps for his head, or cloth, in which he wraps his most treasured feathered ornaments. From eight species he can obtain

INDIANS TAPPING A PALM.

USES OF THE PALM. 137

intoxicating liquor; from many more (not including the cocoa-nut palm, found on the sea-coast) he receives oil and a harvest of fruit; and from one (the *Jará assú*) he procures, by burning the large clusters of small nuts, a substitute for salt. From another he forms a cylinder for squeezing the mandioca pulp, because it resists for a long time the action of the poisonous juice. The great woody spathes of the *Maximiliana regia* are "used by hunters to cook meat in, as, with water in them, they stand the fire well" (Wallace). These spathes are also employed for carrying earth, and sometimes for cradles. Arrows are made from the spinous processes of the *Patawá*, and

THE CAOUTCHOUC-TREE.

lances and heavy harpoons are made from the *Triatea ventricosa;* the long blow-pipe through which the Indian sends the poisoned arrow that brings down the bright birds, the fearless peccari, and even the thick-skinned tapir, is furnished by the *Setigera* palm; the great bassoon-like musical instruments used in the "devil-worship" of the Uaupés are also made from the stems of the palm-trees.

The caoutchouc or gum-elastic tree, called by the natives borracha, and by learned men *Siphilla elastica*, grows to the height of eighty, or even a hundred feet, with a tall, erect stem, a spreading top, and thick glossy foliage. From the stem, when cut, a substance flows, having the appearance of rich yellow cream. This when collected, dried, and blackened in the smoke, is our India-rubber. The natives of Brazil make it into shoes, bottles, toys, &c. Another tree, the massanderuba, yields a white fluid resembling milk, much prized by the natives as a beverage. Here, too, in abundance grows the *Bertholletia excelsa*, a giant tree, which produces the Brazil-nuts which are brought to this country; but we never taste them in perfection, as the fruit is much more delicious when fresh. In the forests are also found the trees which produce vanilla, annato, cacao, cinnamon, &c.

CHAPTER IX.

THE ANIMALS OF BRAZIL.

A River Voyage—Birds and Monkeys—Food of the Natives—Salutation in Brazil—The Jaguar—Its Habits—A Story from Catlin's Travels—The Feast Interrupted—The Disturber Killed—The Tapir—The Anteater—The Iguana—Birds and Insects.

FEW things seem pleasanter (in the description at least) than a voyage at a good season on a Brazilian river. The wild freedom of life in the canoe would of itself be an irresistible attraction to many. The river boats are made so light, that they float gently along the stream. A thatched hut is erected on board, which serves for a house; and sometimes, for a variety, the boat is moored to the shore, and the hammocks of the voyagers are suspended for the night from the branches of a shady tree. For miles and miles unreckoned the river flows on through dark thick forests, shady even at noonday, rich in beauty and ever-changing variety—eye and ear are alike charmed by the luxuriant foliage of the trees, the graceful creepers hanging from bough to bough, and the full song of the many-coloured birds, flitting like bright flowers among the dark green leaves.

Numerous animals inhabit the woods. Flamin-

RIVER-BOAT ON THE AMAZON.

goes, spoonbills, herons, **and waterhens, live** on the banks of the rivers. Monkeys of **all kinds** chatter and whistle in the trees, and flocks **of parrots scream** as their enemies the hawks pursue **them.** Fish and game abound. The natives eat many things that seem strange **food to us.** Their favourite delicacy is the flesh of **the lizard.** They eat also the flesh of the manatee, **or sea cow,** which is like coarse beef. Instead of butter they use an oil made from turtle's eggs, and called turtle-egg butter; and they think a roasted monkey an excellent dish.

Beautiful as is the scenery on **the** banks of **the** Brazilian rivers, the dangerous **currents and other** annoyances spoil the pleasure of the traveller in some degree. **The zancudoes and mosquitoes and** others **of their tribe are a continual** plague. So numerous **and** annoying are **they, that** in some parts of Brazil the morning salutation is not as with us, " How do you do?" or, " It is fine weather to-day;" but, " How did you find the zancudoes during the night?" " How are you to-day **for the** mosquitoes?"

Still worse **than** the mosquitoes, the traveller has to guard also against the attacks of wild and venomous animals. One of the most common of the wild beasts of South America is the jaguar or panther.

The jaguar (*Felis onca*) is an animal of the feline kind; that is to say, it is one of the family of cats. It partakes of the qualities and habits of the tiger; it is a native **of** the hotter parts **of** South America, and, from its being the most formidable quadruped there, it is sometimes called the tiger, **or** panther, of **the new** world. Its colour **is a** pale, brownish yellow, spotted with black. It preys not only on the larger domestic quadrupeds, but also on birds, fish, tortoises, turtles' eggs, &c. The jaguar is an excel-

JAGUAR FISHING.

lent climber, and is equally expert at swimming, so that it is not easy to escape from him. He has been known to climb a tree forty or fifty feet in height in pursuit of monkeys, leaving the mark of his sharp claws on its smooth bark; and he has been also known to swim across a broad and deep river. He catches fish cleverly in the shallows; and when he surprises the turtle asleep on the sand, he turns them neatly on their backs, so that they cannot rise, and then devours them at his leisure.

As an illustration of the stirring nature of a life in the Brazilian forests, we quote a scene from the travels of the celebrated Catlin, whose whole life was spent in exploring woods and wilds, and in becoming acquainted with savage life in all its features. Once, while he was voyaging on the river Trombutas, in Brazil, with a few companions, they were resting on the shore for their mid-day meal. A feast it was to be; for they had killed a wild hog, and determined to have a good banquet. They were roasting it whole, savage fashion, at a fire kindled on the shore. But near them there were natives of the woods, who liked wild hog quite as well as they did, and perhaps thought that these strangers had no right to the game in the wild hunting grounds so long all their own.

However that may be, the panther, the only native lord of the soil, and proprietor of the game, came to see who had been poaching on his manor, attracted by the pleasant odour of the roasting hog. Before he reached the place where the cooking was going on, he found one of the poachers, weary with hunting, asleep on the grass. Not being very hungry, and surprised perhaps at the unusual form of man, my lord panther began to examine the intruder on his territories; and he gently lifted the legs of the sleeping man with his paws, playing with them as his cousin the cat, in her sly and gentle mood, might play with a captive mouse before putting it to death. So this play of the panther would doubtless have ended in the death of the sleeping man, if his danger had not been perceived by his companions. Immediately on seeing it, Catlin hurried from the fire, where their dinner was cooking, to the boat, where he had left his revolver. The head of the panther was behind the body of the sleeping man. Catlin whistled gently; the panther looked up, and received a ball between the eyes, which stretched him lifeless by the side of his intended prey. Imagine the surprise of the sleeper, when, awakened by the shot, he saw how narrowly he had escaped from the jaws of the panther!

The tapir is the largest animal of South America; it forms one of the connecting links between the elephant and the hog. Its snout is lengthened into a kind of proboscis, and, with the exception of the trunk of the elephant, which it resembles, is the longest nasal appendage belonging to any quadruped. It is, however, devoid of that clever little finger with which nature has enriched the trunk of the land leviathan. This curious animal has many fossil relatives, but only three living species (two of them belonging to South America) have as yet been discovered.

The tapir is extensively distributed over South America east of the Andes, but especially abounds in the tropical portions. It seems to be a nocturnal vegetarian,—sleeping during the day, and sallying forth at night, feeds upon the young shoots of trees,

A POWERFUL ANIMAL. 145

buds, wild fruits, maize, &c., &c. It is of a deep brown colour throughout, approaching to black, between three and four feet in height, and from five to six in length. The hair of the body, with the exception of the mane, is scanty, and so closely depressed to the surface, that it is scarcely perceived at a short

THE TAPIR.

distance. Its muscular power is enormous; and this, with the tough, thick hide (almost impervious to musket ball) which defends its body, enables it to tear through thickets in whatever direction it chooses.

The jaguar frequently springs upon it, but is often dislodged by the activity of the tapir, who rushes through the bushes and underwood, and endeavours to brush off his enemy against the thick branches. Its ordinary pace is a sort of trot; but it sometimes gallops, though awkwardly, and with the head down. It is very fond of the water; and high up on the Organ Mountains are pools where it delights to wallow. Its disposition is peaceful, and, if not attacked, it will neither molest man nor beast; but when set upon by the hunter's dogs, it can inflict terrible bites. Mr. Heath informed me that each time it seizes a dog with its teeth, the flesh is cut completely from the bone of the canine intruder. The flesh of the tapir is dry, and is often eaten by the Indians of the interior, by whom it is hunted with spears and poisoned arrows. It takes to the water, and is not only a good swimmer, but appears almost amphibious, being enabled to sustain itself a long time beneath the surface; hence it has sometimes been called *Hippopotamus terrestris*. The largest which Mr. Heath ever shot weighed fourteen Portuguese arrobas (about four hundred and fifty pounds), though, doubtless, much larger exist in the Amazonian regions. Naturalists divide the American tapir into two species,—that of the lowlands, and that of the mountains,—the latter, found on the eastern slopes of the Andes, differing but little from the one already depicted and described.

The peccari is often met with in the woods of Brazil; and this little native swine is the most pugnacious fellow imaginable. Neither men nor dogs inspire reverence, for he will attack both with impunity. It is gregarious in its habits, and will with its companions charge most vehemently, no matter

THE PECCARY.

how great the odds. It is, I believe, one of the very few animals that has no fear of the detonation of fire-arms.

The paca, the capybara, and the agouti, abound in Brazil, and are of the same family as marmots and beavers. The paca attracts the attention of the hunter both on account of the difficulty of its capture (as it takes the water, and swims and dives admirably), and the esculent nature of its flesh. It is about eighteen inches in height, and two feet in length; and its colour is brown spotted with white. The hinder limbs (being considerably bent) are longer than the anterior ones; and its claws are well formed for digging and burrowing. The paca is easily domesticated, and makes a lively pet,—eating readily out of the hand of those it is accustomed to, but hiding from strangers.

The great ant-eater is a most curious animal, but well adapted to the purposes for which it was de-

1. CAPYBARA.   2. AGOUTI.

signed by the Creator. Its short legs and long claws (the latter doubled up when in motion) do not hinder it from running at a good pace; and when the Indians wish to catch it they make a pattering noise upon the leaves as if the rain were falling, upon which the myrmecophaga cocks his huge bushy tail over his body, and, standing perfectly still, soon falls a prey. In the northern part of Minas-Geraes a naturalist once came suddenly upon the great ant-eater, and, knowing the harmless nature of its mouth, seized it by the long snout, by which he tried to hold it, when it immediately rose upon its hind legs, and, clasping him around the middle with its powerful fore paws, completely brought him to a stand. It was struck down with a club a number of times, but soon recovered and ran off; and not until a pistol-ball was lodged in its breast was the naturalist able to add it to his collection. It measured six feet in length without the tail, which, together with the long tufts of hair, measured full four feet more.

GREAT ANT-EATER.

When the great ant-bear sleeps it lies on one side, rolls itself up so that its snout rests on its breast, places all its feet together, and covers itself with its bushy tail. When thus curled up it is so exactly like a bundle of hay that any one might pass it carelessly, imagining it to be a loose heap of that substance.

When it walks or runs the claws of the fore feet are doubled up, causing one side only of the foot to rest upon the ground. The proper use of these powerful claws is to obtain the white ant. When the ant-bear wishes a meal he attacks one of the hard hillocks raised by the ants, and with his huge fore paws furiously tears out a portion of the walls, and thrusting in his long slender tongue, which is covered with a viscid saliva, and to which myriads of ants adhere, he opens his little mouth and draws it in, then, shutting his lips, he pushes out his tongue a second time, retaining the ants in his mouth until the tongue has been completely exserted, when he swallows them. Wallace says that the Indians of the Upper Amazon positively assert that the great ant-eater sometimes kills the jaguar by tightly embracing the latter, and thrusting its enormous claws into the jaguar's sides.

The iguana, a large kind of lizard, is common in Brazil. "In one of my rides towards Canto Gallo," says Mr. Fletcher, "I saw in the road the large lizard called the iguana. There is nothing to me disgusting in this clean-looking reptile, whose skin, composed of bright, small scales, resembles the finest bead-work. I had often seen them at Rio spitted and hawked about the city; for the flesh is esteemed a great delicacy—resembling in its appearance and taste that *bonne bouche* for epicures, a frog's hind leg. The usual pictures of the iguana do not render it full justice; they represent it as horrid in appearance as the imaginary **baleful-breathed**, javelin-tongued dragon, from which good St. George is said to have delivered so many devoted virgins. **The iguana is** from three to five feet in **length, and is oviparous.** A lady member of my family **possessed one** which was a great favourite, **and she** has **kindly** furnished me with some notes on her pet. I insert them verbatim:—

"Pedro (the iguana) afforded me much amusement. From his close resemblance to the snake-tribe, it was difficult for strangers to rid their minds of the impression that he was venomous. Such **is not the** case with iguanas. Their only means **of defence** is their **very** powerful tail, **and a** sportsman **told me** that **he has** had a dog's ribs laid bare by a stroke of an iguana's tail. My poor pet, however, was not warlike, having been long in captivity. He was given me as a 'Christmas-box' by a friend, and soon became tame enough to go at liberty. **He** was about three feet **long,** and subsisted upon raw meat, milk, and bananas. **He had a** basket in my room, and when he felt the weather cool would take refuge between the mattresses of my bed. There, **in** the morning, he would **be** found in all possible comfort. One evening we missed him from all his usual hiding-places, and reluctantly made up our minds that he was lost; but, on rising in the morning, two inches of his tail hanging out **of** the pillow-case told where **he** had passed a snug night! My little Spanish poodle and he were sworn foes. The moment Chico made his appearance, he would dash forward to bite Pedro; but **Chico** thought with many others that the 'better part of valour is discretion.' So he made off from the iguana as fast as his funny legs could carry him. Then Pedro **waddled** slowly back to the sunny spot on the floor and closed his eyes for a nap. When the winter (a winter like the latter part of a northern May) began, he became nearly torpid, and remained without eating for four months. He would now and then sun himself, **but soon return to** his blanket.

"I frequently took **him out on my arm, and he** was **often specially** invited; but I cannot say that he was much caressed. **It** was **in vain that I** expatiated on his beautiful bead-like spots of black and white, on his bright jewel eyes and elegant claws. They admired, but kept their distance. I had a sort of malicious pleasure in putting him suddenly down at the **feet of** the stronger sex, and **I have** seen **him elicit** from naval officers more symptoms of terror than would have been **drawn** forth by an enemy's broadside, or a lee shore. **But alas** for the 'duration of lovely things!' During **the** summer months he felt his old forest-spirit strong within him, and he often sallied forth in the beautiful paths **of** the Gloria. On one of these occasions **he met** a marauding Frenchman. Pedro, the caressed by me and the feared by others, knew no terror. The ruffian struck **him** to the earth. It **was** in vain that a little daughter of Consul B. **tried to** save him by crying, 'Il est à Madame;' another blow fractured his skull! My servant ran up **only in** time to save his body from an ignominious stew-pan; **but** life was extinct. The assassin fled, and Rose came back with **my** poor pet's corpse. On my return he was presented to view with his long forked tongue depending from his **mouth**. He was sent, wrapped in black crape, **to a** neighbour who delighted in fricassed lizard, but who, having seen him petted and caressed, could not find appetite **to eat** him!

" Thus **ended** the career **of** poor **Pedro,** after a **life of** pleasant captivity; and perhaps it might be **said** of him, as of many others, ' He was more feared than loved!' "

The plumage of the birds of Brazil is surpassingly rich and brilliant. From **their** bright-coloured feathers artificial flowers are manufactured of very great beauty. **There are few** curiosities **more** esteemed in Europe and the United States than the feather-flowers of Rio de Janeiro and Bahia. They are made from the natural plumage, though from time to time the novice has palmed off upon him **a** bouquet, the leaves of which, instead of **being** from the parrot, have been stolen from the back of the white ibis and **then** dyed. This deception can, however, be detected by observing the stem of the feather to be coloured green, which is never the case in nature. No ornament can surpass the splendour **of** the flowers made from the breasts and throats **of** humming birds. A lady whose bonnet or **hair is** adorned with such plumage seems to be surrounded with flashes of the most gorgeous and ever-varying brilliancy. The carnations and other flowers made from a happy combination of the feathers of the scarlet ibis and the rose-coloured spoonbill, are also **very natural,** and are highly prized.

154 A BEAUTIFUL DECORATION.

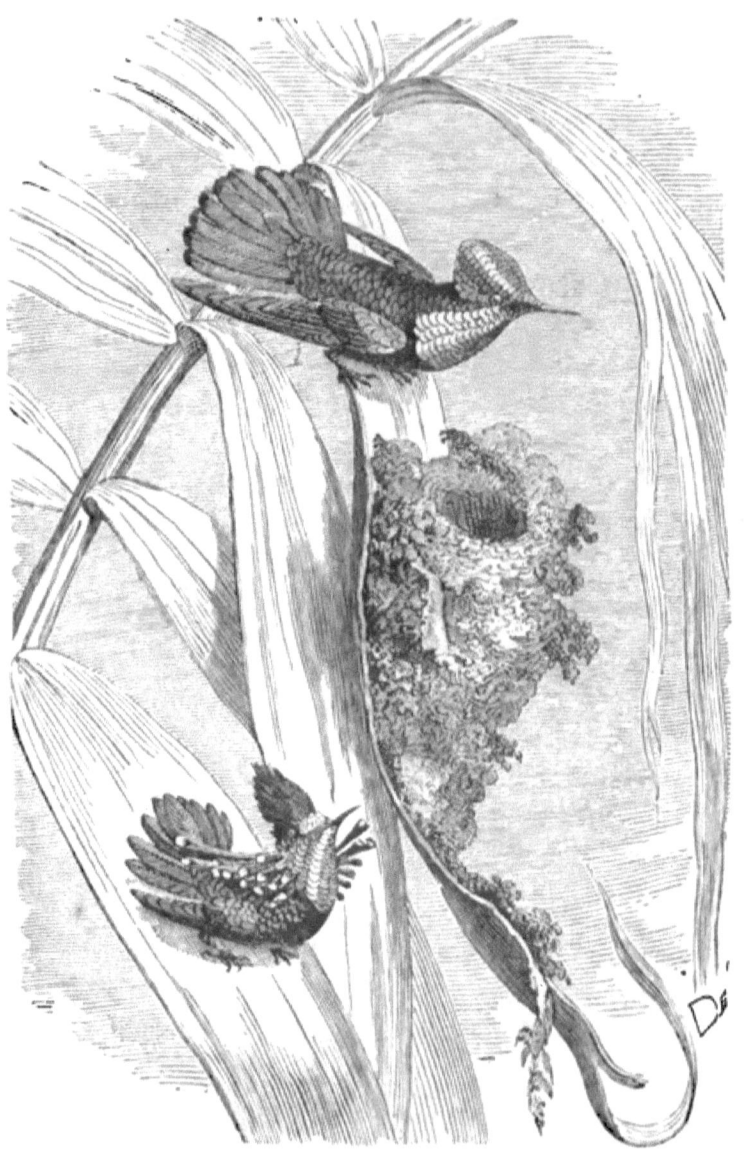

HUMMING BIRDS.

In adorning themselves with these bright feathers the Brazilian ladies have followed the fashions of the native Indians, who have long been accustomed to deck themselves in this way. On the Rio Negro the Uaupé Indians have a head-dress which is in the highest estimation, and they will only part with it under the pressure of the greatest necessity. This ornament consists of a coronet of red and yellow feathers, disposed in regular rows, and firmly attached to a strong plaited band. The feathers are entirely from the shoulders of the great red macaw, but they are not those that the bird naturally possesses, for the Indians have a curious art by which they change the colours of the plumage of many birds. They pluck out a certain number of feathers, and in the various vacancies thus occasioned infuse the milky secretion made from the skin of a small frog. When the feathers grow again they are of a brilliant yellow or orange colour, without any mixture of green or blue, as in the natural state of the bird, and it is said that the much coveted yellow feather will ever after be produced without a new infusion of the milky secretion. Artificial flowers are also manufactured from fish scales and from the wings of insects, and breast-pins are made by setting a small brilliant beetle in gold.

It would require volumes to notice the innumerable brilliant insects that swarm like living gems in the forests of Brazil. At night the fire-flies gleam like stars in the darkness of the deep woods. When caught and imprisoned these little creatures give a brilliant light. " In the mountains of Tijuca," says Mr. Fletcher, " I have read the finest print of *Harper's Magazine* by the light of one of these natural lamps placed under a common glass tumbler, and with distinctness I could tell the hour of the night, and discern the very small figures which marked the seconds of a little Swiss watch. Indians formerly used them instead of flambeaux in their hunting and fishing expeditions, and when travelling in the night they are accustomed to fasten them to their feet and hands. In some parts of the tropics they are used by the senhoritas for adorning their tresses or their robes, by fastening them within a thin gauze-work; and through them their bearers become indeed 'bright particular stars.'"

CHAPTER X.

MINAS-GERAES—ITS **DIAMONDS AND ITS COFFEE**.

Extent of the Province—Its Fertility—Its Minerals—Precious Stones—Diamonds—The Star of the South—Cotton and Coffee—The Native Country of the Coffee Shrub—First Use of Coffee in Europe—The Ancestor of all the American Coffee Shrubs—Comparative Value of Diamonds and Coffee.

THE province of Minas-Geraes is the most important of all the inland divisions of Brazil, owing to its mineral and vegetable riches, its immense herds, its accessibility to market, and its population. It contains 800,000 inhabitants, and yet is so extensive that there are within its area of 150,000 square miles, many forests,—a perfect wilderness, overrun with Indian tribes, and where the jaguar roams in undisturbed independence. Other portions are among the most improved and eligible parts of the empire. One writer has remarked, with great emphasis, that if there be one spot in the world which might be made to surpass all others, Minas is that favoured spot. Its climate is mild and healthful; its surface is elevated and undulating; its soil is fertile, and capable of yielding the most valuable productions; its forests abound in choice timber, balsams, drugs, and dye-woods. But all

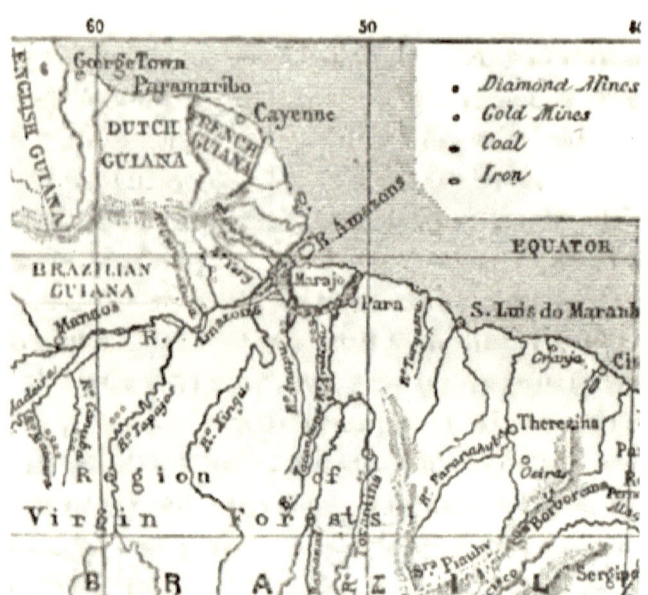

these circumstances together have not given the province so much celebrity as the single fact of its inexhaustible mineral wealth. Its name signifies the general or universal mines, and, accordingly, **mines** of gold, silver, copper, and iron are found **within** its borders, besides quantities of precious stones. Several of **the most** valuable gold-mines not **far** from Ouro Preto **have** been wrought by an English mining company **for** the last twenty years. This enterprise has been unquestionably a source of great profit to its stock-holders, and has rendered great service to the country generally, by introducing the most approved methods of mining, and by giving an impetus to Brazilian industry. This company constantly employs a large number of miners from **Cornwall,** and has established quite an English village at its principal mine.

Amethysts, topazes, emeralds, and other precious stones of great beauty, are found in Brazil; but the most valuable of all its mineral treasures are its beautiful diamonds. They **are** considered less hard and not so fine as those **of** the East Indies, but they are found **in** much greater abundance. They are obtained by washing the sand **in** the beds of the rivers. When uncut it is often difficult to distinguish them from the little pebbles among which they are mixed, but when cut their sparkling brilliancy exceeds that **of** any other stone. When large their value is almost fabulous. The *Star of the South*, a large Brazilian diamond which was shown at the Paris Exhibition, was valued **at** 5,000,000 francs (about £200,000 sterling). It had been found by a negro woman in Brazil; she was a slave,

DIAMOND WASHING—BRAZIL.

as it is in general slaves who are employed in searching for diamonds, and she received her liberty as a reward for her success in finding this rich prize.

The agricultural capacities of the province are very great. It yields coffee, sugar, tobacco, and cotton. It indeed produces some coarse manufactures of cotton. Large quantities of cotton are grown also in other provinces of Brazil. **Pernambuco alone exports more than 6,000,000 pounds of cotton to Liverpool.** In the year 1856 **Great** Britain imported from Brazil 21,830,000 of **cotton.**

The soil of Minas-Geraes yields Indian corn in great profusion, and may be made to grow wheat. Upon its campinas, or upland prairies, innumerable herds of cattle and some flocks of sheep are pastured. The milk of the cows is converted into a species of soft cheese, known as the *queijo* **de** *Minas*. Immense quantities of them may be seen at Rio de Janeiro, and from that port they are scattered along the coast, being very much esteemed as an article of food.

The great staple, however, of Minas-Geraes, **and of** the **whole** empire of Brazil, is **coffee.** What a history might be written of the voyages, **the** naturalization, and the uses of this member of the *Rubiaceæ* family! The coffee-tree is not, as is generally supposed, a native of Arabia, but its home is Abyssinia, and particularly that district called Kaffa, whence the name of the beverage berry.

To this day the coffee-plant is found growing as far as the sources of the White Nile. It **was** not taken **to** Arabia until the fifteenth century, **when,** being cultivated extensively, with great success as to quantity and quality, in the province or kingdom of Yemen, and embarked from Mocha, the coffee of that portion of the world obtained a celebrity which it has never lost. When it was introduced by the Orientals into Europe we know not; but as early as 1538 we find edicts against it, issued by the

Mohammedan priests, on the ground that the faithful went more to the coffee shops than to the mosque. The earliest notice that we have of it in France is in 1643, when a certain adventurer from the Levant established in Paris a coffee-house, which did not succeed. In a few years, however, it became the mode among the aristocracy, through its inauguration by Soliman Aga, the Ambassador of the Sublime Porte at the Court of Louis XIV. Several of the high personages of the time resisted its introduction; among them the celebrated Madame de Sevigné, who had declared that the popularity of coffee would be merely ephemeral; and in the intensity of her admiration for Corneille, she predicted that *La Racine passerait comme le café* (Racine would be forgotten as soon as coffee), both of which predictions have proved rather detrimental to the prophetic reputation of the renowned lady letter writer. Before the middle of the seventeenth century it was in vogue in the principal capitals of Europe. An English merchant from Constantinople was the first to introduce it to the Londoners, and his wife, a young and pretty Greek, was a most attractive saleswoman.

Previous to the eighteenth century, all the coffee consumed in Europe was brought from Arabia Felix, *viâ* the Levant, and the Pachas of Egypt and Syria took good care to increase their coffers by exorbitant transit duties. This exaction was broken up by the vessels of Holland (first), England, and France, sailing round the Cape of Good Hope to Mocha. In 1699, Van Horn, first president of the Dutch East Indies, obtained coffee plants, and had them cultivated in Batavia, where they wonderfully prospered; and the berries of Java obtained a reputation second only to those of Mocha. One of the Batavian shrubs was transplanted to the Botanical Gardens of Amsterdam in 1710, and by great care succeeded so well that a shoot was sent to Louis XIV. and placed in the Jardin des Plantes. From this last plant slips were confided to M. Isambert to be taken to Martinique; but M. Isambert died before the arrival of the ship, and consequently the coffee plants perished. In 1720 Antoine de Jussieu, of the Royal Botanical Gardens, sent, by Captain Declieux, three more coffee shrubs, also destined to Martinique. The voyage was long; the vessel was short of water; two of the plants died; but Captain Declieux shared his ration of water with the surviving coffee plant, and thus succeeded in introducing it into the West Indies; that plant was the ancestor, it is said, of all the coffee plantations in America.

The honour of planting the first coffee-tree in Brazil belongs to the Franciscan friar Villaso, who in 1754 placed one in the garden of the San Antonio convent at Rio de Janeiro. It was not, however, until after the Haytian insurrection that coffee became an object of great cultivation and commerce in Brazil. In 1809 the first cargo was sent to the United States, and all the coffee raised in the empire in that year scarcely amounted to 30,000 sacks, while in the Brazilian financial year of 1855 there were exported 3,256,089 sacks, which brought into the country nearly 25,000,000 dollars. The United States, during the financial year ending June 30,

1856, imported from all coffee-producing countries 235,241,362 pounds of the beverage berry, 180,243,070 pounds (*i.e.*, nearly three-fourths of the whole) of which came from Brazil. The next highest country on the United States' list is Venezuela, which sent them 16,546,166 pounds; and thirdly, Hayti, from which they imported about 13,500,000 pounds. The whole sum paid by the United States for coffee was 21,514,196 dollars, of which Brazil received no less than 16,091,714 dollars.

The great coffee region is on the banks of the Rio Parahiba, and in the province of San Paulo; but every year it is more widely cultivated, and a considerable quantity is now grown in provinces further northward. It can be planted by burying the seeds or berries (which are double), or by slips. The trees are placed six or eight feet apart; and those plants which have been taken from the nursery with balls of mould around their roots will bear fruit in two years; those detached from the earth will not produce until the third year, and the majority of such shrubs die. In the province of San Paulo, and the richest portions of Minas Geraes, 1000 trees will yield from 2560 to 3200 pounds; in Rio de Janeiro, from 1600 to 2560. In some parts of San Paulo, 1000 trees have yielded 6400 pounds, but this is extraordinary. In the province of Rio de Janeiro, trees are generally cut down every fifteen years. There are some *cafiers* on the plantation of Senator Vergueiro which are twenty-four years old, and are still bringing forth fruit. As a general rule, they are not allowed to exceed twelve feet in height, so as to be within reach. When the berry is ripe, it is about the size and colour of a cherry, and resembles it, or a large cranberry; of these berries a negro can daily collect about thirty-two pounds. There are three gatherings in the year, and the berries are spread out upon pavements or a level portion of

COFFEE PLANTATION.

ground (the *terreno*), from whence they are taken when dry, and denuded of the hull by machinery, and afterward conveyed to market. Nothing is more beautiful than a coffee plantation in full and virgin bloom. The snowy blossoms all burst forth simultaneously, and the extended fields seem almost in a night to lay aside their robe of verdure, and to replace it by the most delicate mantle of white, which exhales a fragrance not unworthy of Eden. But the beauty is truly ephemeral, for the snow-white flowers and the delightful odour pass away in twenty-four hours.

It is by toilsome journeys on mule-back that the coffee sacks from Minas-Geraes generally reach a market, and nothing so much hinders the general prosperity of this province as its lack of good roads and some feasible thoroughfare to a market. The province has of late years expended considerable sums upon the construction of roads, but as yet it cannot send a single ton of its produce to market upon wheels. The journey from Ouro Preto, the capital, to Rio de Janeiro, a distance of about 200 miles, is performed on the backs of mules and horses only, and ordinarily requires fifteen days.

It is instructive to look at the widely different results of the mineral and vegetable riches of the empire. After Mexico and Peru (before the discovery of Australian and Californian treasure), Brazil furnished the largest quantum of hard currency to the commercial world. Here the diamond, the ruby, the sapphire, and the topaz, and the rainbow-tinted opal, sparkle in their native splendour. And yet, so much greater are the riches of the agricultural productions of the empire, that the annual sum received for the single article of coffee surpasses the results of eighty years' yield of the diamond mines. From 1740 to 1822 (the era of independence), a period which was the most prosperous in diamond mining, the number of carats obtained were 232,000, worth not quite £3,500,000 sterling. The exports of coffee from Rio alone during the year 1851 amounted to £4,756,794! And when we add the sums obtained for the other great staples of sugar, cotton, seringa (or the India-rubber), dye-woods, and **the productions of the immense herds of the South, we have, it is true, a better** idea of the sources of wealth in **Brazil, but only a** faint conception of the vast re-**sources of this fertile empire.**

CHAPTER XI.

SELVAS OF THE AMAZON.

Extent of the Selvas—Night in the Forest—Death-like Stillness—Roar of Wild Beasts—Wild Chorus at Dawn—A Thunder Storm—A Primeval Forest and its Inhabitants—Large Locust Trees—Wonderful Fig-tree—Rosewood Trees.

The Selvas or Forest Plains of the Amazon, lying in the centre of the continent, form the second division of the North American lowlands. This country is more uneven than the Pampas, and the vegetation is so dense that it can only be penetrated by sailing up the river or its tributaries. The forests not only cover the basin of the Amazon from the Cordillera of Chiquitos to the mountains of Parima, but also its limiting mountain-chains the Sierra dos Vertentes and Parima, so that the whole forms an area of woodland six times the size of France, lying between the eighteenth parallel of south latitude and the seventh of north—consequently intertropical and traversed by the equator. There are some marshy savannahs between the third and fourth degrees of north latitude, and some grassy steppes south of the Pacasaimo chain; but they are insignificant compared with the Selvas, which extend 1500 miles along the **river,** varying in breadth from 350 to 800 miles. According **to** Humboldt, the soil, enriched for ages by the spoils of the forest, consists of the richest mould. The heat is suffocating in the deep **and** dark recesses of these primeval woods, where not **a** breath **of** air penetrates, **and where, after** being drenched **by** the periodical rains, the damp **is so excessive that a blue** mist rises in the early morning **among** the huge stems of the **trees, and** envelops the entangled creepers, stretching from bough to bough. A death-like stillness prevails from sunrise to sunset, then the thousands **of** nocturnal animals that inhabit those forests **join in** one loud discordant roar, **not continuous, but in** bursts. **The beasts seem to be** periodically **and** unanimously roused by **some unknown** impulse, till the forest rings in universal uproar. Profound silence prevails at midnight, which is broken at the dawn of morning **by** another **general** roar of wild chorus. The whole forest often resounds **when** the animals, startled from their sleep, scream **in** terror at the noise made **by bands of its** inhabitants flying from some night-prowling **foe.** Their anxiety and terror before a thunder-storm is excessive, and all nature seems to partake in **the** dread. The tops **of** the lofty trees rustle ominously, though not a breath **of** air agitates them; a hollow whistling in the high regions **of** the atmosphere comes **as a** warning from the black floating vapour; midnight darkness envelops the ancient forests, which soon after groan and creak with the blast of the hurricane. The gloom is rendered still more hideous by the vivid lightning **and the** stunning crash of thunder. Even fishes are affected with the general consternation, for in a few minutes the Amazon rages in waves like a stormy sea.

These primeval forests are interspersed with open patches of grass and marsh lands, similar in character to the llanos and prairies. The woods are composed of large trees of various sizes and heights, and differing greatly in species. On a space of twenty square yards there may be found thirty or forty trees, all of different species. The intervals between the trees are filled up with grass, shrubs, and bushes of various kinds and sizes, the whole being closely interlaced and matted together by numerous climbing plants and creepers, thus forming a woody fabric quite impenetrable to the foot of man. In this mass of tangle and underwood a few small openings appear, through which the jaguar and other wild beasts find access to the beds of the rivers. These immense forests are populated by monkeys in incredible number, and of various species, which are hunted by the natives, who dry and eat their flesh. Birds of various kinds, and of every variety of plumage, are seen along the banks of the rivers. This is the grand region of serpents, some of which are venomous.

This region deserves, in the strictest sense of the word, to be called a primeval forest, a term that has, in recent times, been so frequently misapplied. Primeval or primitive, as applied to a forest, a nation, or a period of time, is a word of rather indefinite signification, and generally but of relative import. If every wild forest, densely covered with trees, on which man has never laid his destroying hands, is to be regarded as a primitive forest, then the phenomenon is common to many parts both of the temperate and the frigid zones; if, however, this character consists in impenetrability, **through which** it is impossible to clear **with** the axe, between **trees** measuring from eight to twelve feet in diameter, **a path of any length,** primitive forests belong exclusively **to tropical regions.** This impenetrability **is** by **no** means, as it **is** often erroneously supposed **in** Europe, always occasioned by the interlaced climbing "lianes," or creeping plants, for these often constitute but a very small portion of the underwood. The chief obstacles are the shrub-like plants which fill up every space between **the trees, in a zone** within which **all** vegetable **forms have** a tendency to become aborescent.

The Picture represents a part of the trunk of one of the great locust-trees which are to be seen in the old woods of Brazil. They are thus described by the traveller Von Martius:—

"The place where these prodigious trees were found appeared to me as if it were the portals of a magnificent temple, **not** constructed by the hands of man, but by God himself, as if to awe the mind **of** the spectator with a holy dread of his own presen**ce.** Never before had I beheld such enormous trunks,— they looked more like living rocks than trees; for it was only on the pinnacle of their bare and naked bark that foliage could be discovered, and that at such a dis**tance** from the eye that the forms of the leaves could **not** be made out. Fifteen Indians with outstretched arms could only just embrace one of them. At the bottom they were eighty-four feet in circumference, and sixty feet where the boles became cylindrical." By counting the concentric rings of such parts as were accessible, he arrived at the conclusion that they were of the age of Homer, and 332 years old in the days of Pythagoras. One of his estimates reduced their age to 2052 years, while another

THE GREAT LOCUST-TREE.

carried it up to 4104; from which he argues that the trees cannot but date far beyond the time of our Saviour. Their colossal appearance is well shown in the picture, a small portion of the lower part of the trunk only being represented.

Very large trees are also to be seen in other parts

A WILD FIG-TREE.

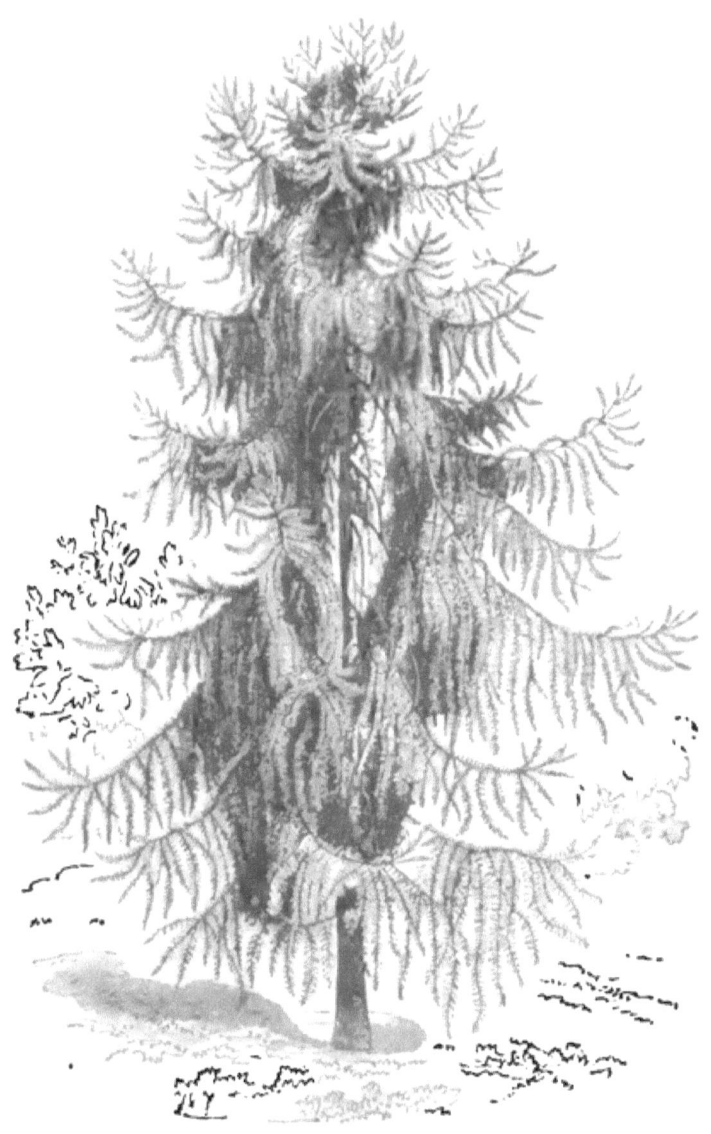

BRAZILIAN PINE.

of Brazil. At a place called Padre Corréar, not far from Petropolis, is a celebrated wild fig-tree, whose branches extend over a circumference of 480 feet; and 4000 persons, it is computed, can stand under its shade at noon-day. Near by, on the height east of the hamlet, can also be seen two rows of the Brazilian pine (*Araucaria Braziliana*), so well known in the large conservatories of Europe and the United States. When 100 miles further in the interior, I saw many jacarandá (rosewood) trees. Their resemblance to the common locust of the United States is very striking. There are a number of species of the jacarandá, varying in tint from a deep rich brown to a beautiful violet. The latter kind I have never seen north of the equator, save in small specimen-pieces; but at the Fayenda de Governo, Dr Joaquin A. P. Da Cunha, the amiable proprietor, showed me, in his establishment for making sugar, a beam, fifty feet long and three feet in diameter, of the violet-tinted jacarandá. It had performed the menial office of a connecting beam for fifty years, and its exterior was dusty; but, on chipping it, I found it to be of the most beautiful violet. The wood of Dr. Da Cunha's pig-pen consisted of boards and sticks of rosewood; but let none of my readers imagine a highly-polished piano or a splendid centre-table; for exposure to the atmosphere renders the jacarandá as plebeian in appearance as the commonest weather-beaten pine. The rosewood-tree is cut down, deprived of its branches, and conveyed to market generally by floating it to some seaport-town, whence it is shipped to North America and Europe. It is exceedingly hard and durable, cog-wheels made of this wood lasting longer than those constructed from any other ligneous substance. The United States annually purchase of Brazil 80,000 dollars worth of rosewood.

CHAPTER XII.

THE RIVER AMAZON, AND THE STORY OF MADAME GODIN DES ODONNAIS.

Course of the Amazon—Its Tributaries—Its Various Names—First Discovery—Expeditions of Orellana and Teixeira—Voyage of Madame Godin des Odonnais—Her Sufferings—Death of all her Companions—Ten days alone in the Forest—Her Meeting with the Indians—Arrival at Cayenne—Return to France.

"Where can we find on the surface of the globe a river equal to the mighty Maranon or Amazon, that giant among the rivers of the earth, gathering its waters from a surface of a million and a half square miles, and bearing them to the ocean after a course of nearly 3000 miles? This mighty monarch receives in his progress the homage of tributaries, each of which, by its greatness, and the abundance of its waters, would suffice for the wants of a whole vast country. Such are the Ucayah, the Rio Purus, the Rio Negro; above all, the Madera, rivalling in importance the river to which it yields the honour of giving a name to their united waters. The further it advances in its majestic course, the more its proportions increase; and before arriving at the ocean, its broad sheet, from the middle of which the eye cannot reach the banks, seems rather to be a fresh water sea, flowing sluggishly towards the ocean basin, than a river of the continent.

"This noble stream, which exceeds in magnitude the largest rivers in the Old World, takes its rise from two sources, the one of which is found in the glaciers of Lauricocha (one of the loftiest of the Cordillera range); the second in the snowy summit of Mount Cailloma, in the same lofty chain. Swelled by the tributary streams of the Yupura and the Rio Negro on the left bank, and by the Yavari, the Yutay, and the Yurna, the Mugua, the Rio de los Capanachuas, and the Pachira on the right, it flows for a long period through the mountain gorges of prodigious depth and surpassing beauty. After emerging from the Andes, it winds in a lazy current through the immense savannahs of South America, and does not reach the ocean till it has run a course of 315 leagues after its junction with the Rio Negro. From its source to the sea is 1035 leagues or 2700 miles. Its breadth, after it emerges into the plain, is generally from two to three miles, and its depth is seldom less than eighty fathoms. After its junction with the Xuaga, however, its expanse becomes so great that in mid-channel the opposite coasts can hardly be seen; and it flows in a vast estuary, so level, that the traces of the tide are seen at the distance of 250 leagues from the sea coast. A vehement struggle ensues at its mouth, between the river flowing down and the tide running up; twice every day they dispute the pre-eminence, and animals equally with men withdraw from the terrible conflict. In the shock of the enormous masses of water, a ridge of surf and foam is raised to the height of **180 feet;** the islands **in** the neighbourhood are shaken in **the** strife; the fishers, the boatmen, and **the** alligators withdraw trembling from the shock. At spring-tide such **is** the vehemence **of this** collision, that the opposite waves precipitate themselves **on** each **other like** hostile armies; **the shores are** covered **to a** great distance on either **sides** with volumes of foam; huge **rocks,** whirled about like barks, are borne aloft on the surface; and the awful roar, re-echoed from island to island, gives the first warning to the far distant mariner that he is approaching the shores of South America."

A volume of **fresh water,** constantly replenished **by** copious rains, **pours** forth with **such** impetus as **to** force itself — an unmixed current — into the ocean, **to** the distance of eighty leagues. While the principal branch of the Ganges discharges 80,000 cubic feet of water every sixtieth part of a minute, the Amazon sends through the Narrows at Obidos 550,000 cubic feet per **second;** while the whole area drained by the Mississippi **and its** branches, is 1,200,000 square miles, the **area** of the Amazon and its tributaries (not including that of the Tocantins, which is larger than the **Ohio** Valley), is 2,330,000 square miles. This is more than a third of all South America, and equal to two-thirds of all Europe. Mr. Wallace has startled Englishmen with the fact, that "all Western Europe could be placed in it without touching its boundaries, and **it** would even contain the whole of our Indian Empire."

This " King **of** waters " **is** remarkable for its wide spreading tributaries, which are nearly all navigable to a great distance, from their junction with the main trunk, and, collecting the whole, afford an extent of water communication unparalleled in any other part of the globe. There is a total of ten thousand miles of steam navigation below all falls; and, these obstructions once passed, steamers could be run for four thousand miles.

The native name of Amazon is "Para," which signifies "the father of waters." It has been also called "Maranon" from the Portuguese words, meaning "not the sea" (as it appears to be near its mouth); "Orellana" from the name of the Spaniard Orellana, who was the first to descend the stream to its mouth; and "Amazon," because the Spaniards believed that the first natives who met them in battle on its shores were women. Later travellers have said that this fancy originated in the feminine appearance of the Indians of that country, who wear their hair in long locks, sometimes plaited, or fastened up with a comb—and who adorn themselves with bracelets and necklaces. The use of ornaments in these tribes is almost confined to the men.

The first expedition of Orellana took place in 1541–42, and the second in 1544. About seventy years afterwards the Portuguese began to settle in Para. In 1616 the foundations of the present city of Para were laid by Francisco Cadeira. In 1637 another party descended the Amazon from Quito, and in the same year the first expédition for the ascent of the Amazon was organized. It was commanded by Pedro Teixiera, and was composed of 70 soldiers, 1200 native rowers and boatmen, besides females and slaves, **who** increased the number to about 2000. They embarked in forty-five canoes. After a voyage of eight **months** the remains of the party (many of whom had deserted) reached the extent of navigation. There the commander left his canoes **and** continued his journey overland **to** Quito, **where** he was received with distinguished honours. After this voyages upon the Amazon became more common.

In 1745, Mr. La Condamine, a French Academician, descended from Quito, and constructed a map of the river, based upon a series of astronomical observations. His memoir, read before the **Royal** Academy **on** his return, remains to **this day a very** interesting work. In modern times the most **celebrated** voyages down the Amazon have been described at length by those who accomplished them,—*e.g.* Spix, and Von Martius, Lister Maroc, Lieutenants Smith, Herudon and Gibbon, and Mr. Wallace. The expeditions to which I have alluded have generally been prosperous, and not attended with **any** peculiar misfortunes. Not so with every voyage that has been undertaken upon these interminable waters. The sufferings of Madame Godin des Odonnais have hardly a parallel on record. The husband of this lady was **an** astronomer associated with M. Condamine. **He** had taken his family with him to reside in Quito, **but** being ordered to Cayenne, was obliged **to** leave them behind. Circumstances transpired **to** prevent his returning for a period of sixteen years, **and** when finally he made the attempt to ascend the Amazon, he was taken sick and could not proceed. All the messages that he attempted to send his absent wife failed of their destination. In the meantime a rumour reached her that an expedition had been despatched to meet her at some of the missions on the upper Amazon. She immediately resolved to set out on the perilous journey. She was accompanied by her family, including three females, two children, and several men, two of whom were her brothers. They surmounted the Andes and passed down the tributary streams of the Amazon without serious difficulties; but the further they entered into the measureless solitudes that lay before them, the more their troubles increased. The missions were found in a state of desolation under the ravages of the small-pox. The village where they expected to find Indians to conduct them down the river had but two inhabitants surviving. These had no boat, but they engaged to construct one and pilot it to the mission of Andoas, about twelve days journey below, descending the river of Bobonaza, a distance of from 140 to 150 leagues; she paid them beforehand. The canoe being finished, they all departed from Canelos. After navigating the river two days, on the succeeding morning the pilots absconded; the unfortunate party embarked without any one to steer the boat, and passed the day without accident.

The next day at noon they discovered a canoe in a small port adjoining a leaf-built hut, in which was a native recovering from illness, who consented to pilot them. On the third day of his voyage, while stooping over to recover the hat of Mr. R. which had fallen into the water, the poor man fell overboard, and, not having sufficient strength to reach the shore, was drowned. Behold the canoe, again without a steersman, abandoned to individuals perfectly ignorant of managing it. In consequence, it was shortly overset, which obliged the party to land and build themselves a hut. They were now but from five to six days' journey from Andoas. Mr. R. proposed to repair thither, and set off with another Frenchman of the party, and the faithful negro belonging to Madame Godin, taking especial care to carry his effects with him. "I since blamed my wife," says her husband who related the story, "for not having despatched one of her brothers to accompany Mr. R., but found that neither of them, after the accident which had befallen the canoe, were inclined to trust themselves on the water again without a proper pilot. Mr. R., moreover, promised that within a fortnight a canoe should be forwarded to them with a proper complement of natives. The fortnight expired, and even the five and twenty days, when giving over all hopes, they constructed a raft on which they ventured themselves, with their provisions and property. The raft, badly framed, struck against the branch of a sunken tree, and overset, all their effects perishing in the waves, and the whole party being plunged into the water. Thanks to the little breadth of the river at this place, no one was drowned, Madame Godin being happily saved, after twice sinking, by her brother. Placed now in a situation still more distressing than before, they collectively resolved on tracing the course of the river along its banks. How difficult an enterprise this was, any one may be aware, who knows how thickly the banks of the river are beset with trees, underwood, herbage, and lianas, and that it is often necessary to cut one's way. They returned to their hut, took what provisions they had left behind, and began their journey. By keeping along the river's side, they found its sinuosities greatly lengthened their way, to avoid which inconvenience they penetrated the wood, and in a few days they lost themselves. Wearied with so many days' march in the midst of woods, incommodious even for those accustomed to them, their feet torn by thorns and brambles, their provisions exhausted, and dying with thirst, they were fain to subsist on a few seeds, wild fruit, and the palm cabbage. At length, oppressed with hunger and thirst, with lassitude and loss of strength, they seated themselves on the ground without the power of rising, and, waiting thus the approach of death, in three or four days, expired one after the other. Madame Godin, stretched on the ground by the side of the corpses of her brothers and other companions, stupified, delirious, and tormented with choking thirst, at length assumed resolution and strength enough to drag herself along in search of the deliverance which providentially awaited her. Such was her deplorable condition, she was without shoes, and her clothes all torn to rags. She cut the shoes off her brother's feet, and fastened the soles on her own. It was about the period between the 25th and 30th of December 1769, that this unfortunate party (at least seven of the number of them) perished in this miserable manner; the date I gather by what I learn from the only survivor, who related that it was nine days after she quitted the scene of the wretched catastrophe described before she reached the banks of the Bobonaza. Doubtless, this interval must have appeared to her of great length; and how a female so delicately educated, and in such a state of want and exhaustion, could support her distress, though but half the time, appears most wonderful. She assured me that she was ten days alone in the wood, two awaiting death by the side of her brothers, the other eight wandering at random. The remembrance of the shocking spectacle she witnessed, the horror incident on her solitude, and the darkness of night in a desert, the perpetual apprehension of death, which every instant served to augment, had such an effect on her spirits as to cause her hair to turn grey. On the second day's march, the distance necessarily inconsiderable, she found water, and the succeeding day some wild fruit and fresh eggs of what bird she knew not, but which, by her description, I conjecture to have been a species of partridge. These with the greatest difficulty was she enabled to swallow, the aesophagus, owing to the want of aliment, having become so parched and straitened; but these and other food she accidentally met with sufficed to support her skeleton frame. At length, and not before it was indispensable, arrived the succour designed for her by Providence. Were it told in a romance that a female of delicate habit, accustomed to all the comforts of life, had been precipitated into a river; that, after being withdrawn when on the point of drowning, this female, the eighth of a party, had penetrated into unknown and pathless woods, and travelled in them for weeks, not knowing whither she directed her steps; that enduring hunger, thirst, and fatigue to very exhaustion, she should have seen her two brothers, far more robust than her, a nephew yet a youth, three young women her servants, and a young man, the domestic left by the physician who had gone on before, all expire by her side, and she yet survive; that, after remaining by their corpses two whole days and nights, in a country abounding in tigers and numbers of dangerous serpents, without once seeing any of these animals or reptiles, she should afterwards have strength to rise and continue her way, covered with tatters, through the same pathless woods for eight days together, till she reached the banks of the Bobanaza, the author would be charged with inconsistency; but the historian should paint facts to his reader, and this is nothing but the truth.

It was on the eighth or ninth day, according to Madame Godin, after leaving the dreadful scene of the death of her companions, that she found herself on the banks of the Bobanaza. At daybreak she heard a noise at about two hundred paces from her. Her first emotions, which were those of terror, occasioned her to strike into the wood; but, after a moment's reflection, satisfied that nothing worse could possibly befall her than to continue in her present state, and that alarm was therefore childish, she proceeded to the bank of the river, and perceived two native Americans launching a boat into the stream. It is the custom of these people, on their landing to pass the night, to draw their canoe either wholly, or partially on shore, as a security against accidents; for, should it be left afloat, and the fastening tackle break, it would be carried away by the current, and leave the sleepers on shore in a truly helpless state. The natives, perceiving Madame Godin, advanced towards her, on which she conjured them to transport her to Andoas. They had been driven by the contagion prevalent at Canelos, to withdraw with their wives to a hut they had at a distance, and were then going to Andoas. They received my wife on board with kindness truly affectionate, showed every attention to her wants, and conducted her to that village.

At Andoas Madame Godin procured a canoe, with a crew from the village, and thus reached Laguna, where she remained six weeks to rest after her dreadful journey—having travelled upwards of four hundred leagues. She had yet four or five times that distance to pass before she reached Cayenne, but she refused to return. The rest of her journey was performed in comparative comfort on board a Portuguese vessel. She met her husband again after their long separation, and, as soon as her health would permit, she accompanied him to Europe. Not all the care and tenderness lavished on her by her husband would make her lose the remembrance of her fearful sufferings in the forest, and long after she was settled in her quiet and pleasant home on their estate at St. Amand in Berry, she shuddered at the slightest word which reminded her of her travels; and the sudden mention of South America or the Amazon would cause a nervous fit, which deprived her of her voice, and left her for hours pale, cold, silent, plunged in deep thought and still deeper melancholy.

Steam navigation has now begun on the Amazon.

In 1857 there were seven steamers in successful operation, and two new boats were expected. If this enterprise succeeds as it ought to do, flourishing cities and cultivated fields may soon replace the wild forest; and the jaguar and the alligator may be gradually exterminated as their haunts are taken possession of by civilized man.

CHAPTER XIII.

PLANT AND ANIMAL LIFE ON THE AMAZON.

The Turtle of the Amazon—Turtle Egg Butter—Indian way of Catching Turtle—Indian Shooting—The Umbrella Bird—The Victoria Regia—The Jacana—The Fish-Cow—The Anaconda—A Horse Swallowed by a Snake—Narrow Escape from a Boa Constrictor.

"THE tartaruga, or turtle, of the Amazons are to be found by the thousand in nearly all the affluents, especially the Madeira, Purus, Napo, Ucayali, and Huallaga. At the season for them to deposit their eggs on the '*praias*,' the streams will be fairly speckled with them, paddling their clumsy carcases up to their native sand-bar, for it is positively asserted by the natives that the turtle will not deposit its eggs anywhere except where it was itself hatched out. They lay from 80 to 120 eggs every other year. Of this I have been assured by persons who have artificial ponds, and keep them the year round for their own table. September and October are the months for depositing their eggs."

Dr. Kidder says:—

"The *turtle-egg butter* of Amazonia (*manteiga da tartaruga*) is a substance quite peculiar to this quarter of the globe. At certain seasons of the year the turtles appear by thousands on the banks of the rivers, in order to deposit their eggs upon the sand. The noise of their shells striking against each other in the rush is said to be sometimes heard at a great distance. Their work commences at dusk, and ends with the following dawn, when they retire to the water.

"During the day-time the inhabitants collect these eggs and pile them up in heaps resembling the stacks of cannon balls seen at a navy yard. These heaps are often twenty feet in diameter, and of a corresponding height. While yet fresh they are thrown into wooden canoes, or other large vessels, and broken with sticks and stamped fine with the feet. Water is then poured on, and the whole is exposed to the rays of the sun. The heat brings the oily matter of the egg to the surface, from which it is skimmed off with cuyas and shells. After this it is subjected to a moderate heat until ready for use. When clarified, it has the appearance of butter that has been melted. It always retains the taste of fish-oil, but is much prized for seasoning by the Indians and those who are accustomed to its use. It is conveyed to market in earthen jars. In earlier times it was estimated that nearly 250,000,000 of turtles' eggs were annually destroyed in the manufacture of this manteiga. Recently the number is less, owing to the gradual inroads made upon the turtle race, and also to the advance of civilization."

But the Government now regulates the turtle egg harvest, so that their numbers may not be so rapidly diminished. There are some extensive beaches which yield 2000 pots of oil annually. Each pot contains five gallons, and requires about 2500 eggs, which would give **5,000,000 ova** destroyed in one locality.

Indeed, it is a wonder how the turtles can ever come to maturity; as they issue from the eggs, and make their way to the water, many enemies are awaiting them. Huge alligators swallow them by hundreds; the jaguars feed upon them; eagles, buzzards, and great wood-ibises are their devourers; and when they have escaped these land foes, many ravenous fishes are ready to seize them in the stream. They are, however, so prolific, that it has remained for their most fatal enemy, man, to visibly diminish their number. The Indians take the full-grown turtle in a net, or catch him with a hook, or shoot him with an arrow. The latter is a most ingenious method, and requires more skill than to shoot a bird upon the wing. The turtle never shows its back above the water, but, rising to breathe, its nostrils only are protruded above the surface; so slight, however, is the rippling, that none but the Indian's keen eyes perceive it. If he shoot an arrow obliquely, it would glance off the smooth shell; therefore he aims into the air, and apparently "draws a bow at a venture;" but he sends up his missile with such wonderfully accurate judgment, that it describes a parabola and descends nearly vertically into the back of the turtle.—(*Wallace*.) The arrow-head fits loosely to the shaft, and is attached to it by a long, fine cord, carefully wound round the wood, so that when the turtle dives the barb descends, the string unwinds, and the light shaft forms a float or buoy, which the Indian secures, and by the attached cord he draws the prize up into his canoe. Nearly all the turtles sold in the market are taken in this manner, and the little square, vertical hole made by the arrow-head may generally be seen in the shell.

In connection with this might be mentioned the archery of some of the civilized Indians in various

THE UMBRELLA BIRD.

portions of the empire. A large and strong bow is bent by their legs. In this way they are able to shoot game at a great distance.

As to the birds of the Amazon, they are every-

INDIAN MODE OF SHOOTING.

where brilliant beyond birds in any other portion of the world. Some, like the dancing cock of the rock and the curious little-known umbrella bird, are very difficult to obtain. I can only mention the latter.

This singular bird is about the size of a raven, and is of a similar colour, but its feathers have a more scaly appearance, from being margined with a different shade of glossy blue. On its head it bears a crest different from that of any other bird. It is formed of feathers more than two inches long, very thickly set, and with hairy plumes curving over at the end. These can be laid back so as to be hardly visible, or can be erected and spread out on every side, forming, as has been remarked, " a hemispherical or rather a hemi-ellipsoidal dome, completely covering the head, and even reaching beyond the point of the beak." It inhabits the flooded islands of the Rio Negro and the Solimões, never appearing on the mainland. It feeds on fruits, and utters a loud, hoarse cry, like some deep musical instrument—whence its Indian name, Ueramimbé, "trumpet bird."

Near the margin of the Amazon and its tributaries is found the giant of Flora's kingdom, whose discovery a few years since is as notable a fact to the naturalist world as the regular opening of steam navigation upon the Amazon is to the commercial world.

Of all the Nymphæaceæ, the largest, the richest, and the most beautiful, is the marvellous plant which has been dedicated to the Queen of England, and which bears the name of Victoria Regia. It inhabits the tranquil waters of the shallow lakes formed by the widening of the Amazon and its affluents. Its leaves measure from fifteen to eighteen feet in circumference. Their upper part is of a dark, glossy green; the under portion is of a crimson red, furnished with large salient veins, which are cellular

VICTORIA REGIA.

and full of air, and have the stem covered with elastic prickles. The flowers lift themselves about six inches above the water, and when full blown have a circumference of from three to four feet. The petals unfold toward evening; their colour, at first of the purest white, passes in twenty-four hours through successive hues, from a tender rose tinge to a bright red. During the first day of their bloom they exhale a delightful fragrance, and at the end of the third day the flower fades away and replunges beneath the waters, there to ripen its seeds. When matured, these fruit-seeds, rich in fecula, are gathered by the natives, who roast them, and relish them thus prepared.

In 1845 an English traveller, Mr. Bridges, as he was following the wooded banks of the Yacouma, one of the tributaries of the Mamoré, came to a lake hidden in the forest, and found upon it a colony of Victoria Regias. Carried away by his admiration, he was about to plunge into the water for the purpose of gathering some of the flowers, when the Indians who accompanied him pointed to the savage alligators lazily reposing upon the surface. This information made him cautious; but, without abating his ardour, he ran to the city of Santa Anna, and soon obtained a canoe, which was launched upon the lake which contained the objects of his ambition. The leaves were so enormous that he could place but two of them on the canoe, and he was obliged to make several trips to complete his harvest. Mr. Bridges soon arrived in England with the seeds, which he had sown in moist clay. Two of these germinated in the aquarium of the hothouse of Kew. One was sent to the large hothouses of Chatsworth; a basin was prepared to receive it, the temperature was raised, and the plant was placed in its new resting-place on the 10th of August 1849. Toward the end of September, it was necessary to enlarge the basin and to double its size, in order to give space to the leaves which developed with great rapidity. So large did they become that one of them supported the weight of a little girl in upright position.

The first bud opened in the beginning of November. The flower in bloom was offered by Sir J. Paxton (the celebrated designer of the London Crystal Palace) to his monarch, and the great personages of England hastened to Windsor Castle to admire the beautiful namesake of their gracious sovereign.

The name given to this marvellous plant by Lindley was happily chosen; but the natives of Amazon call it " Uapé Japona "—the Jacana's oven —from the fact that the jacana is often seen upon it. The jacana is a singular spur-winged bird, twice the size of a woodcock, provided with excedingly long and slender toes (from which the French term it the surgeon-bird) which enable it to glide over various water-plants. It inhabits the marshes and woods near the water, and many a time in the interior I have seen it stealing over the lily leaves on the margin of rivers.

The waters of the great river are scarcely less productive than the soil of its banks. Innumerable species of fish and amphibious animals abound in it. Several kinds of fish are salted and dried for use; but the commerce in this article of food does not extend beyond the coast. Owing to the style of preparation, or to the coarse quality of the fish, foreigners set no value upon it. The most remarkable inhabitant of these waters is the *vaca marina*, commonly called by the Portuguese *peixe boi*, or fish cow. This name is evidently given on account of the animal's size, rather than from any resemblance to the ox or cow other than its being mammiferous.

THE VACA MARINA, OR FISH-COW.

The *vaca marina* cannot be called amphibious, since it never leaves the water. It feeds principally upon a water-plant (*cana brava*) that floats on the borders of the stream. It often raises its head above the water to respire, as well as to feed upon this vegetable. At these moments it is attacked and captured. It has only two fins, which are small, and situated near its head. This has been pronounced the largest fish inhabiting fresh water; but, notwithstanding its mammoth dimensions,—being, according to various accounts, from eight to seventeen feet long, and two or three feet thick at the widest part, —its eyes are extremely small, and the orifices of its ears are scarcely larger than a pin-head. Its skin is very thick and hard, not easily penetrated by a musket-ball. The Indians used to make shields of it for their defence in war. Its fat and flesh have always been in estimation. It served the natives in place of beef. Not having salt for the purpose, they used to preserve the flesh by means of smoke.

The following account of the multitude of fish in the Rio Madeira, a tributary of the Amazon, is given by Mr. Nesbitt, chief engineer in one of the Government steamers:—" At the falls of the Rio Madeira the traveller will halt and gaze with wonder at the vast multitude of fish of all kinds and sizes—from the huge cow-fish to the little sardine— struggling with might and main to ascend the foaming, dashing current, without the slightest hope of success. Presently some monster will make a dash at a school of his small congeners, when suddenly there will be a cloud of all sorts and sizes leaping in the air, and trying to dodge their ravenous pursuer. All that is necessary for one wishing a fish is to take his canoe paddle and strike right or left, when he is sure to hit—he cannot possibly miss. Here are almost always to be found great numbers of Indians collecting, salting, and drying fish. The *peixe boi* is an excellent fish for food. I would almost as soon have it for the table in every shape as the best veal; indeed, it might be palmed upon the unwary for that article. It is also equal to the best dried beef in the estimation of many."

The enormous anaconda (*Eunectes murinus*), or sucurujú of the natives, a serpent belonging to the boa family, inhabits tropical America, and particularly haunts the dense forests near the margin of rivers. The boa-constrictor, the jiboa of the Indians, is smaller and more terrestrial. The first of these creatures which I saw, says Mr. Fletcher, was a young one, belonging to a gentleman in the province of St. Paulo. I afterwards saw one in the province of Rio de Janeiro, that measured twenty-five feet. Mr. Nesbitt, the engineer who took the Peruvian Government steamers to the upper affluents of the Amazon, informed me that he shot on the banks of the Huallaga an anaconda which measured twenty-six feet seven inches. An Italian physician at Campinas (St. Paulo) gave me an account of the manner in which the sucurujú, or anaconda, took his prey.

The giant ophidian lies in wait by the river-side, where quadrupeds of all kinds are likely to frequent to quench their thirst. He patiently waits until some animal draws within reach, when, with a rapidity almost incredible, the monster fastens himself to the neck of his victim, coils round it, and crushes it to death. After the unfortunate animal has been reduced to a shapeless mass by the pressure of the snake, its destroyer prepares to swallow it, by sliming it over with a viscid secretion. When the anaconda has gulped down a heifer (by commencing with the tail and hind feet brought together), he lies torpid for a month, until his enormous meal is digested, and then sallies forth for another. The doctor added that the sucurujú does not attempt the deglutition and digestion of the horns, but that he lets them protrude from his mouth until they fall off by decay. It had been said by some casual observers that the anaconda dies after swallowing a large

ANACONDA KILLING DEER.

animal,—that the buzzards seen near him eat him up; but the doctor added that close observation shows that this statement was entirely erroneous.

As to the amount of credence due to the statements of Dr. B., relative to the horns of the swallowed animal, I leave the reader to form his own opinion; but the facts are incontrovertible in regard to the capacity of the anaconda to swallow animals whose diameter is many times greater than its own. Of all the travellers and explorers whose writings I have read, Wallace and Gardiner are the most moderate in their account as eye-witnesses, and are most particular to record nothing of which they were not fully persuaded after patient and careful investigation. Mr. Wallace says, "It is an undisputed fact that they devour cattle and horses."

In the province of Goyaz, Dr. Gardiner came to the fazenda of Sapé, situated at the foot of the Serra de Santa Brida, near the entrance to a small valley. This plantation belonged to Lieutenant Lagoeira. Dr. G. remarks, that in this valley and throughout this province the anaconda attains an enormous size, sometimes reaching forty feet in length,—the largest which he saw measured thirty-seven feet, but was not alive. It had been taken under the following circumstances:—

"Some weeks before our arrival at Sapé," writes Dr. Gardiner, "the favourite riding horse of Senhor Lagoeira, which had been put out to pasture not far from the house, could not be found, although strict search was made for it all over the fazenda. Shortly after this, one of his *vaqueiros* (herdsmen) in going through the wood, by the side of a small stream, saw an enormous sucurujú suspended in the fork of a tree which hung over the water. It was dead, but had evidently been floated down alive by a recent flood, and being in an inert state, it had not been able to extricate itself from the fork before the waters fell. It was dragged out to the open country by two horses, and was found to measure thirty-seven feet in length. On opening it, the bones of a horse, in a somewhat broken condition, and the flesh in a half-digested state, were found within it; the bones of the head were uninjured. From these circumstances we concluded that the boa had swallowed the horse entire. In all kinds of snakes the capacity for swallowing is prodigious. I have often seen one not thicker than my thumb swallow a frog as large as my fist; and I once killed a rattlesnake about four feet long, and of no great thickness, which had swallowed not less than three large frogs. I have also seen a very slender snake that frequents the roofs of houses swallow an entire bat three times its own thickness. If such be the case with these smaller kinds, it is not to be wondered at that one thirty-seven feet long should be able to swallow a horse, particularly when it is known that previously to doing so it breaks the bones of the animal by coiling itself round it, and afterwards lubricates it with a slimy matter, which it has the power of secreting in its mouth."

On one occasion, when the sailors from a French ship landed on the coast of Brazil, one of them had a very narrow escape from a boa, which is thus related in the narrative of their adventures:—

"One day the captain and his adopted son had landed on the coast, and were admiring the glorious trees, and the rich plumage of the birds which were flitting among them, when they heard on a sudden

SAILOR SEIZED BY A BOA.

screams and cries of distress, as if from some one in agony. They knew that one of the sailors had landed when they did, as they intended to cut wood for fuel; but they could scarcely believe that the cries were his, for what could have happened to him in such a short time?

"Richard, with the activity natural to his age, began to run at once to the quarter whence the cries came. He soon outstripped the captain, although he was running too; and when he reached the place where they had left the sailor, he found him in torture. His face expressed the extreme of agony, his eyes were starting from his head, his hair was standing on end. An enormous serpent, about twenty feet in length, was coiled round his body, and was squeezing him in its folds, so that he could scarcely breathe.

"When the courageous boy saw the fearful state of the poor sailor, he hesitated not a moment, but rushing towards the venomous creature with his axe in his hand, he seized the moment when its great head was near him to give it a blow with all his strength. The monstrous head was bent downwards for a moment by the force of the blow,— Richard soon followed it by another, and another, and at length he succeeded in crushing the enormous head. The animal, mortally wounded, losing its strength and its power of injuring, let go by degrees the body of the sailor, who was thus saved from the very jaws of death.

"One long hiss announced the death-throes of the monster, 'Well done, my boy!' said the captain, laying his hand on Richard's shoulder; 'very well done! Yours is true courage.'

"'Richard,' said the rescued sailor, offering him his hand, "you have saved me from a terrible death, my life henceforward is yours."

"Richard and the sailor continued close and constant friends to their lives' end."

CHAPTER XIV.

THE MINES OF UPPER PERU.

Situation and Productions of Bolivia—Maize—*Chicha*—*Quinoa*—*Coca*— Description of the *Coca* Bush—Cultivation and Uses—Silver Mines of Potosí—Discovery of the Mine.

BOLIVIA, or Upper Peru, is, next to Thibet, the highest country in the world. It was separated from Peru in 1825, and takes its name from its liberator—Bolivar. It is a plateau situated to the north of Chili, between two parallel chains of the Cordilleras. It is nine times the size of England, and has a population of 1,600,000, three-fourths of whom are Indians.

In Bolivia the Andes are broad and high, and form two ranges, enclosing between them a lofty valley, in the north of which is the large lake Titicaca, 12,846 feet above the ocean. At such a height the soil is, of course, cold and barren—the icy winds descending from the snowy tops of the Andes, and, sweeping over the plains, hinder the growth of vegetation. But in the deep and numerous valleys which intersect the plateau, the soil produces in abundance all the grains and fruits of Europe, which were introduced **by** the Spaniards **at** the time of the conquest, and also sugar canes, cotton, bananas, &c.

Maize and potatoes form the principal food of the poorer classes. They eat the maize both roasted and boiled, **and are** passionately fond of a drink which **they make from it** called *chicha*. This *chicha* is **the chief** beverage **of** the country, and contains, **it is** said, so much nourishment, that the natives can live on it for a long time without any other food. Those who habitually drink the *chicha* become **so** fat that they are scarcely able to **walk.**

There is a peculiar kind of grain which **has been** given by Providence to this country, **as it ripens at a** very great height above the level of **the sea,** where neither barley nor oats could thrive,—this **is the** *quinoa*, **a** small plant, of which **the** seeds are eaten, boiled or cooked in various ways, and whose leaves are used as vegetables, and also serve to make a kind of beer. There is another plant of this country which is still more appreciated by the inhabitants, and which is **the** friend and consolation of the Indian in every trial and difficulty of his life. This is the *coca*. While he chews his coca-leaves, **the** poor native forgets all his miseries, his rags, and the cruel treatment of his master. He requires **but a** single meal in the day, but he needs **to** stop **his** work at least three times in order to chew **his** coca. He believes that it both strengthens him and prolongs his life, and that it is, besides, a valuable antidote to the bad effects of the rarity of the air **in** these mountainous regions.

The coca is a bush which attains the height of

six or eight feet, and resembles the black-thorn in its small white flowers and bright green leaves. It is a native of the tropical valleys on the eastern slope of the Andes, and grows wild in many parts of these countries. That which is used by the people, however, is chiefly the produce of cultivation. In the inhabited parts of the valleys it forms an important agricultural crop. Like our common thorn it is raised in seed-beds, from which it is planted out into regularly arranged coca plantations. The steep sides of the valleys, as high up as eight thousand feet above the level of the sea, are often covered with these plantations of coca. The leaves are about the size of those of the cherry-tree, and, when ripe enough to break on being bent, they are collected by the women and children, and dried in the sun. Their taste is not unpleasant; it is slightly bitter and aromatic, and resembles that of green tea of inferior quality. It becomes more piquant and agreeable when a sprinkling of quicklime or plant-ashes is chewed along with it.

The use of this plant among the Indians of South America dates from very remote periods. When the Spanish conquerors overcame the native races of the hilly country of Peru, they found extensive plantations of coca. The beloved leaf is still, to the Indian of the mountains, the delight, the support, and, in some measure, the necessity of his life.

A confirmed chewer of coca is called a "coquero," and he is said to become occasionally more thoroughly a slave to the leaf than the inveterate drunkard is to spirituous liquors.

The chewing of coca gives a bad breath, pale lips

and gums, greenish and stumpy teeth, and **an ugly black mark** at the angles of the mouth. The inveterate "coquero" is known at the first glance,— his unsteady gait, his yellow skin, his dim **and** sunken eyes, encircled by **a** purple ring, his quivering lips, and his general **apathy,** all bear evidence of the **baneful effects of the** coca juice when taken in excess.*

Regions so little attractive as the cold and rugged plateaux of Bolivia might have possibly been destitute of inhabitants had they not possessed an extraordinary number of rich gold **and** silver mines. These are often found at **a** very great elevation, sometimes as high as the top of the European **Alps;** and **round these** the population **have gathered and** founded cities. **Potosi,** the highest **city in the** world, stands **at** an elevation of 13,330 **feet, at** the foot **of a** mountain celebrated for its silver mines. The top of the mountain rises **to a** height of 15,200 feet, and is pierced with more than 300 **shafts.** Since **its** discovery in 1846, these have produced the **almost** fabulous sum **of** 8,000,258,000,000 of francs, chiefly **in silver.**

The mountain **of Potosi** is very steep, of a conical **form,** and is about three **miles** in circumference. **It is** pierced in every direction; the passages of **the** mines are supported by 300 large arches **of** columns, which, with innumerous furnaces which surround it, offer **a** brilliant spectacle at night. **It** has been the tomb **of** many thousands of men, **as** for **a** long time 15,000 **persons** were constantly

---

* From "Chemistry of Common Life."

obliged to work there. The veins are now much less productive than formerly.

The town of Potosi is situated in a barren country, with a cold climate around it; nothing is to be seen but bare rocks, here and there covered with moss. The surrounding mountains, inhabited only by a few vicuñas and condors, have their summits covered with perpetual snow. Strangers who are not accustomed to the climate often suffer much from the rarity of the air. The population of the town has been naturally regulated by the prosperity of the mines. In 1611 it amounted to about 160,000; but of late years, since the mines were less productive, it has not much exceeded from 10,000 to 12,000. The discovery of the most important mines has often been owing to circumstances quite unexpected, and sometimes very strange. Many singular stories are told about these discoveries, not the least remarkable of which relates to the finding of the celebrated mine of Potosi. It is said that an Indian, named Diego Hualea, when scrambling up the mountains, seized hold of a shrub to support himself; it yielded under his weight, was torn up by the roots, and displayed to the eyes of the astonished hunter a mass of silver, of which some pieces were mingled with the earth which was clinging to the roots of the shrub. The Indian made use privately of this inexhaustible treasure; but his good fortune did not remain long concealed, for his friend Quanca having remarked a great change in his way of life, became curious to know the reason of it. He entreated Hualea to tell him, and succeeded in winning from him the secret of his

SILVER MINES OF POTOSI—PERU.

riches. For some time this secret was well kept, but Hualea having refused to teach his friend the way to purify the metal, Quanca told the whole story to Villareas, his master, who resided at Porco.

Villareas immediately went to examine the place on the 21st of April 1545; the mine was opened, and has continued to be worked ever since.

Another curious story is told of the discovery of the celebrated silver mines of Pasco, which are situated on the south-east of the lake of Lauriocha, one of the sources of the great river Amazon.

About two hundred and thirty years ago an Indian was keeping the flocks of his master on a little plain situated in these high regions. One day, having wandered further than usual from his hut, he felt bitterly cold. He took shelter under a high rock, and kindled a good fire to warm himself, near which he fell asleep. Great was his surprise on awaking to find that the stone on which he had kindled the fire was melted and changed into pure silver. He immediately hastened to tell his master of this strange adventure. Without losing a moment, Ugarte (for so the Spaniard was called) accompanied his shepherd to the favoured spot, and discovered the existence of an extremely rich vein of silver, which he hastened to work, and from which he derived immense revenues. This valuable mine is not yet exhausted. No sooner had the news of this event become known in the country, than a great number of the inhabitants of Pasco, only two leagues distant, hastened to the spot, sought, and found new veins. This mine was so rich that it has collected and maintains a population of 18,000.

The ground upon which Cerro de Pasco has been built resembles a fine net-work of silver veins. If a hole is dug almost anywhere, silver is almost certain to be discovered. Some of the inhabitants are even said to work a private mine in the cellars of their houses. But the mining is, in general, done both irregularly and imprudently, in consequence of which the shafts and galleries often fall in and bury the unfortunate Indian miners under heaps of earth and stones. In the mine of Matagente alone, now entirely destroyed, more than 300 workmen have lost their lives. It is well named, as the word Matagente means literally *kill people.*

It is said also that, in another part of America, a poor Spaniard, entirely destitute and flying from justice, was one day swimming across a river to escape from the alguazils who were in pursuit of him. Just as he reached the opposite bank of the river, his eyes fell upon a vein of silver in the rock, which had been laid bare by the constant action of the water on the bank. He understood at a glance all the advantages that he might gain from this discovery; and without delay he hastened to return to his native place, surrendered himself to justice, and submitted to the sentence pronounced against him. Then, after a certain time of imprisonment, he went back to the place where he had discovered the vein of silver, and began the working of a mine, which soon made him one of the richest proprietors in the country.

Several of the mines in the Upper Cordilleras have yielded silver to an almost incredible amount. One of these was the mine of *San José,* in the department of Huanvélica, in Peru. The proprietor of this mine requested his friend, the Spanish governor Castro, to be the godfather of his first child. The viceroy, not being able to be absent from his post, sent his wife in his stead. The proprietor of San José caused the road between his house and the church (not a short distance) to be laid with a triple row of ingots of silver; and, on the departure of the vice-queen, he presented to her all the silver that had been used in making this singular avenue, as a testimony of his gratitude for the honour she had done him.

The poor Indians were not long in finding out that they gained nothing by the discovery of the mines, since they were obliged to labour very hard, and received almost nothing for their work; and it often cost them their lives. It is said that this was the fate of the Indian who first discovered the mine of Cerro de Pasco; for his master, Ugarte, so far from being grateful to him for his valuable information, threw the poor man into a dungeon, where he died. Therefore, although the existence of numerous veins of silver was known to several Indians, they did all they could to guard the secret from the knowledge of Europeans. Such secrets were often transmitted from father to son for a long course of years.

A Franciscan monk, of Huanacayo, who was an incorrigible gambler, and always short of money, had yet gained the affection of the Indians by his kindness and good nature to them; and they very often brought him small presents of cheese and poultry. One day, that he had lost a large sum of money at play, he made **known his** difficulties **to an** Indian in whom he had confidence. **This** man **promised** to help him; and the next evening he brought him a sack filled with the richest silver ore. This present was several times repeated; but the insatiable monk was still anxious **for** more, and entreated **the** Indian **to** tell **him** where **he got** so much treasure. **After being often asked, the Indian** yielded at length to his importunities. He went one night, accompanied **by** two others, to the Franciscan's house, bandaged his eyes, took him upon his shoulders, and, being assisted in carrying him by his companions **in turn,** he conveyed him to a considerable **distance among** the mountains. **At** length **he** set **him** down, **unbound** his **eyes, and told** him **to look.** The monk found himself **in a small shaft, of** no great **depth;** but his eyes **were** perfectly dazzled with **the** riches surrounding him. His curiosity being satisfied, he was permitted to fill a sack as well as he could, and his eyes having been again bandaged, he **was** conveyed home in the same way in **which** he had come. **As** he **was** carried along, **he dropped** from time to time a bead of his rosary, hoping that by means of these **he** might be able next **day** to trace the way to the mine. But two hours had scarcely passed after he had gone to bed, dreaming of untold riches, **when his** brilliant visions were disturbed by his guide: "**My** father," said the Indian quietly, "**you** have lost **your** rosary!" and, **so** saying, he handed to the **monk a** handful of his beads.

CHAPTER XV.

PERU.

Extent and Productions—Guano—Dangers of Travelling—Poisoned Springs—Storms among the Mountains—Peruvian Bridges—Encounter with a Tiger—Wonderful Escape.

PERU, a country in South America, lying north of Bolivia (which at one time formed part of it), is composed of high table-land, having, on one side, immense forests and grass-covered plains, and, on the other, towards the Pacific Ocean, a skirting of barren, sandy shores. The vegetation is not so luxuriant as in some other parts of America, although the watered valleys, orange-trees, bananas and citrons as large as oaks, are not uncommon, Indian corn, varieties of wheat, the finest potatoes in the world, and excellent tapioca, are extensively cultivated. These, however, are not the productions which we usually associate with the name of Peru. The word calls up ideas of rich mines of gold and other metals; and it is true that for many centuries this country furnished Spain with fabulous revenues. But things have changed; and many of our readers will hardly believe that the guano which fleets of ships carry away from its shores **is immensely more valuable** than all the **gold and silver mines in its** possession.

Every evening, at sunset, innumerable multitudes of frigate-birds, petrels, gannets, pelicans, &c., may be seen perched **on the rocks** which border **the small islands or shores of** this part of America; **and the** droppings **and** other remains of these birds, mixed with masses of decayed fish, form the guano, which **is** one of the richest manures known, and much sought after by agriculturists, both in England and the United States. It **is** found **in** greatest abundance on the Chincha Islands, **off the coast of** Peru, where the deposits **are sometimes twenty and** thirty feet thick; **and** this natural wealth, which **costs** nothing but the trouble **of** gathering and carrying away, has yielded to Peru *about two millions*, while the exportation **of** metals has scarcely exceeded *a third of the sum*. When we remember how necessary manure **is** for agriculture, we can understand why enterprizing men go to the other side of the globe in search of it, **and why it is more valued** in our day than the productions of gold **mines.**

Even that part of Peru which lies along the coast is very hilly. The valleys are little more than **ravines,** and the rivers are impetuous torrents, rushing in numberless cascades towards the sea. But however difficult or dangerous a journey in the maritime provinces may appear, it is only an agreeable promenade compared with an excursion into the interior. Along the shores there is nothing to be feared but fatigue, the sun, the sand, and robbers; but **an** expedition **to** the mountains includes such a variety of dangers, which even the natives shrink from encountering, that it is difficult to conceive where travellers could be found willing to brave them. When such a journey is undertaken, the traveller must be prepared to risk his life at almost every step, and to depend on the providence of God for protection and deliverance. Dangers from avalanches, precipices, and glaciers are common to all mountainous countries; but, besides these, travellers in the Andes have to guard against peculiar diseases—even the loss of sight.

Dr von Tschudi, well known by his remarkable work on the Alps, relates that, one day after a long journey through one of the valleys leading from the sea to the mountains, he stopped to refresh himself and his mule at a spring, and was in the act of drinking, when an Indian called out, "Take care!—that water is poisoned!" and, to his disappointment, he was compelled to remount without having tasted it; for, if he had done so, he would certainly have had an attack of fever, and perhaps have died in consequence.

At some places the valley which we passed through, says Dr. von Tschudi, was merely a narrow cleft between two precipitous rocks, 500 or 600 feet high, whose summits sometimes inclined and touched each other, so as to form a kind of natural arch. A narrow and dangerous path, watered by the foaming waves of a torrent, ran along their base, or rather their steep sides. When not quite perpendicular, the slopes were covered with threatening masses of rock, which, becoming gradually loosened, often fall into the valley, driving everything before them. While passing through this ravine, one of these immense blocks rolled down, and, striking one of my mules, threw him into the torrent, carrying away my instruments, some of my principal travelling utensils, and part of my papers and collections; and, in the inn at Viso, I met an officer, who told me he had set out from San Matéo, riding with his two sons, the one before and the other behind him, and, when about six miles from Viso, a piece of rock fell down, and, striking the eldest, a child of ten years old, plunged him into the torrent.

But these are not the only dangers which travellers in the high regions of the Cordilleras have to fear. At the height of 9000 or 10,000 feet above the level of the sea, they experience the most painful sensations—are often seized with fainting and bleeding at the eyes, nose, and mouth. This malady is called *puna* by the natives, and *veta* or *mareo* (from its resemblance to sea sickness) by the Spanish creoles, who in their ignorance attribute it to the exhalations from metals; but the real cause is to be found in the rarefaction of the air.

Another disease is the *surumpe*, a violent inflammation of the eyes, caused by the reflection of the sun upon the snow. In these regions the rarity of the air and the violence of the wind keep the eyes in a state of constant irritation. The sky becomes suddenly darkened with clouds, which is followed by a heavy fall of snow; the clouds disappear as quickly as they came, and the sun shines out again in all its brilliancy. Almost immediately the traveller feels an acute pain in his eyes, as if a fire burned within. The eyes become red, the eyelids swell and bleed, and the pain becomes so intense that delirium comes **on,** and is **in** many instances followed by death. Spectacles and green veils **are** an excellent precaution against this malady.

During five months in the year, from November **to March,** scarcely a day passes without **a storm on** these mountains. It commences almost invariably **between** two and three o'clock in the afternoon, and continues till five or half-past five, and never later **than six.** Generally a good deal of snow falls while it lasts, but the sun of **the** following **day rapidly** thaws it. For several **hours the flashes of** lightning follow so rapidly upon one another **as** to tinge **the** mountain cataracts with the hue of blood. The thunder rumbles incessantly, and the lightning flashes along the ground, leaving long furrows in the burned grass behind it. The traveller overtaken by these terrific tempests is glad to leave his frightened mule to herself, and seek a shelter under some overhanging rock.

But we must not forget in our enumeration of the dangers of a journey in Peru the suspension bridges and *huaros.* The bridges are constructed of four thick strips of cow hides, which are fastened to posts, fixed on the banks of the river or torrent. A plaiting of smaller strips, covered with branches of trees, straw, and roots, is laid upon these. Two other strips, placed at about three feet high, serve for balustrades, and the traveller, leading his stubborn mule by the bridle, is obliged to cross upon **this** unsteady platform, which swings like a hammock, often at a great height above the water. The crossing of a river in a huaros is still more unpleasant. A rope is stretched from one bank to the other, to which a rough wooden seat is fastened, and by the aid of a second rope the seat with the travellers on it is drawn across. If the rope should happen to break, he will to a certainty be drowned.

Sometimes the two banks of a torrent are so very close to one another, that travellers who have confidence in their mules leap over at the risk of their lives.

Dr. von Tschudi had also dangers to fear from encounters with wild beasts. One day, on the very spot where he was going to sit down, he discovered, and at last succeeded in killing, a little black serpent, whose sting is said to be so very poisonous that it is useless to try any remedy. Another time a gigantic condor pounced upon a sheep which had just been killed, and tried to carry it off, and the doctor had considerable difficulty in defending himself with his hatchet. On another occasion his life was threatened by a tigress, and it was entirely owing, under Providence, to his composure and presence of mind that he was enabled to preserve it. Fatigued, he says, by a long journey, he had just sat down under the shade of a tree, laying his musket, which was his constant companion, by his side. Suddenly his eyes fell upon some plants which he had not seen before, and on rising to examine them with all the enthusiasm of a botanist, his attention was attracted by a rustling among the leaves of the trees. He turned round to find out the cause, and suddenly a tigress, with two cubs playing about her, started up between him and the tree where he had left his weapon. At sight of him the wild animal stopped, and uttered a dull kind of roar; the little cubs stopped at the same time, as if astonished at the novelty of the object. Dr. T. knew that a tigress never appears so formidable as when she requires to defend her young; and finding himself without arms, confronted with such a terrible animal, a shudder of terror passed over him, and for an instant he gave himself up to despair; but soon recovering his courage and presence of mind, he resolved to try the power of his eyes, and fixing them upon those of the tigress, endeavoured to hinder her from advancing. Strange to say, the expedient succeeded beyond all his expectation, and the animal, as if riveted to the spot, did not come one single step nearer. But her cubs, not knowing the danger, darted forward, and gambolled about his legs. The sight of this disturbed the tigress, which began to roar and lash her sides violently with her tail, ready to rush upon the traveller if he dared to touch her little ones. At that instant the doctor, still keeping his eyes upon the mother, stooped down, and passing his hand over the back of the young tigers, who seemed to appreciate the caress as much as if they had been little kittens, noticed that the ferocious animal was not insensible to the marks of regard lavished on her offspring. Her growling ceased, and she resumed her attitude of calm curiosity. The two cubs, impelled by their playful and frolicsome humour, darted off again from the traveller, biting and chasing each other, and straying beyond sight or hearing of their mother. She became anxious about them, and turned her head slowly as if inclined to follow them. Taking advantage of this moment, Dr. T. got behind a bush, which concealed him from the tigress, and by a short detour reached the place where he had left his gun, and prepared to use it if necessary against the formidable inhabitant of the forest. But it was in vain that he followed on her track; tigers and tigress had disappeared, and it may be believed that he did not much regret their absence.

CHAPTER XVI.

THE THREE REPUBLICS:—ECUADOR, NEW GRANADA, AND VENEZUELA.

Description of the Country—Earthquakes—Productions—Pearl Fishery—Value of Pearls—Pearl Divers—Dangers and Labours of the Divers—A Shark Overhead.

ANCIENT Colombia, which occupied in the northwest of South America all the territory between the Isthmus of Panama and Peru, is now divided into three independent republics,—that of Venezuela, of which we shall afterwards speak; that of New Granada, to the south of the Isthmus; and that of Ecuador, or the Equator, the name of which sufficiently indicates its geographical position.

The greater part of the country in the two last mentioned states is singularly steep and hilly, rent by deep ravines, so difficult to cross, that it is impossible in many places to make any kind of road for beasts of burden, and rich people are accustomed to travel seated in chairs carried on men's backs. With this heavy burden the hardy mountaineers scramble up terrific precipices and across frightful ravines, which but for them would be quite inaccessible.

BRIDGES OF ICONOZO.

CHAPTER XVI.

THE THREE REPUBLICS:—ECUADOR, NEW GRANADA, AND VENEZUELA.

Description of the Country—Earthquakes—Productions—Pearl Fishery—Value of Pearls—Pearl Divers—Dangers and Labours of the Divers—A Shark Overhead.

ANCIENT Colombia, which occupied in the northwest of South America all the territory between the Isthmus of Panama and Peru, is now divided into three independent republics,—that of Venezuela, of which we shall afterwards speak; that of New Granada, to the south of the Isthmus; and that of Ecuador, or the Equator, the name of which sufficiently indicates its geographical position.

The greater part of the country in the two last mentioned states is singularly steep and hilly, rent by deep ravines, so difficult to cross, that it is impossible in many places to make any kind of road for beasts of burden, and rich people are accustomed to travel seated in chairs carried on men's backs. With this heavy burden the hardy mountaineers scramble up terrific precipices and across frightful ravines, which but for them would be quite inaccessible.

BRIDGES OF ICONOZO.

There are several remarkable natural wonders to be seen amidst the bold and picturesque scenery of this country. Such, for example, as the celebrated bridges of Iconozo, formed by enormous blocks of rock, which have fallen across a ravine 125 yards in depth, through which rushes a foaming torrent. One of these bridges, situated a little lower down than the other, is formed of three enormous rocks, which have fallen so as mutually to support each other, the middle one forming a kind of keystone to the natural arch.

In another place, one of the rivers of this country —the Rio de Bogota—throwing itself into one of the ravines common in this part of the Andes, forms the waterfall of Téquendama, one of the most beautiful in the world, which falls a height of at least 230 yards, and is always crowned with a column of vapour, which is seen at the distance of more than twelve miles.

Another cause of wonder and fear to the traveller in these regions are the numerous and terrible volcanoes, whose eruptions have often caused the most dreadful devastation. In 1797 a whole district, to the extent of 125 miles in length, and 88 in breadth, was literally torn up and entirely desolated. Forty thousand persons lost their lives at Quito and in the neighbouring cities. At the time of the eruption of 1803, the sudden melting of the snows which covered the summit of Cotopaxi caused terrible devastation. In 1768 the ashes of this volcano darkened the air to a distance of 65 miles. At another time the flames rose 1000 yards in height above the crater; and on other occasions its terrible roaring was heard **at** 120 miles, or even 480 miles distance. **If** it were **not** that man gets accustomed to everything, even to the **most** dreadful dangers, **no** one could live in this country without suffering **from** constant terror **and alarm.**

The climate **of** the high plateaux, situated on the equator, **ought to have the** pleasant temperature of **perpetual** spring, **and such** was formerly the reputation **of the** city of Quito, in particular; but it appears that this is much modified in consequence of the terrible earthquakes which have marked the end of the last century. In the plains which lie on the sea-coast, or at the foot of the mountains, **the heat in** summer is often stifling, the climate unhealthy, and yellow fever frequent.

The principal productions of this country **are excellent cocoa,** vanilla, bark, tobacco, indigo, cotton, **several** kinds **of** balm, and lastly, the cow-tree, from which flows, when it is cut, a white and abundant beverage, of an agreeable taste, not unlike milk.

The mines furnish **a small** quantity of gold, silver, platina, emeralds, **known by** the name of Peruvian emeralds, salt, and a little quicksilver.

The population, which is not very numerous, **is** composed of whites, of Spanish origin, of Indians, placed in a dependent position, although not actually slaves, half-bloods, and a small number of negroes.

The principal cities of the Republic of Ecuador are Quito, the capital of the state, said to contain 70,000 inhabitants, **situated** about 9540 feet above the level of the **sea, in a** country which produces the best cocoa in the world—and Guayaquil, a busy

The age of a common oyster can be told by counting the successive layers of plates overlapping each other. These are technically called "shoots," and each of them makes a year's growth, so that it is easy to know how long the creature has lived. When the oyster is young, the "shoots" are regular and successive, but as it gets old they become irregular, and are piled over one another.

The increase of the shell of the pearl oyster probably takes place in the same way.

The number of oysters which contain pearls, or at least pearls of any value, is comparatively small; but the shells of all are of some use, as they are all lined with a substance of the same nature as pearls, called mother of pearl, of which buttons, the handles of penknives, small boxes, paper knives, and various other articles and toys are made. The outer or coarser parts of the shell are taken off by means of sharp cutting instruments, or with a file, and the inner layers are then formed into many ornamental trifles.

The most valuable pearls are those which are perfectly round or pear shaped. In Europe white pearls are preferred, but in the East they prefer the yellow, the pink, or the black; the last are extremely rare. A fine necklace composed of pearls about the size of a pea, would cost from about £150 to £300; but a necklace of pearls about the size of grains of pepper might not cost more than from £15 to £20.

One of the most celebrated pearls is one in the crown of Spain, which was given to King Philip II. It was oval, and of the size of a pigeon's egg, and was valued at 80,000 ducats. A pearl which Pliny valued at about £100,000 of our money, Cleopatra is said to have dissolved at a banquet, where she drank it off to Anthony's health, not **to be** outdone by him in extravagance.

In Panama every **person** in easy circumstances has two **or three negroes, or** Indians, who **dive to procure pearls for their** masters. These divers, **trained** to **the** trade **from** their earliest years, are **sent to** the islands **of** the bay, where tents and boats are kept in readiness for them. Eighteen or twenty of the poor creatures, good swimmers, and able to hold in their breath, are placed under the orders **of** an inspector, and they go out **to** sea in the boats, till they reach **a place where** there **is a bed of oysters at a depth of not** more than ten, **twelve, or** fif**teen** fathoms.

When they have fixed on a favourable spot, they cast anchor; the negroes, or Indians, fasten a rope round their bodies, and load themselves with a small weight to enable them to go down more easily. They then throw themselves **into** the water, and when they reach the bottom **they** tear off the oysters. They take one under each arm, one in each hand, and a fifth in the mouth, and, thus loaded, they ascend again to take breath and throw the oysters into the boats. As soon as they have taken breath they dive again, and so continue till **they are** quite exhausted, or till they think that they have collected a sufficient number of oysters.

Their task ended, each negro opens his own oysters in the presence of the inspector, and gives him all the pearls, small or great, perfect or imperfect, which they contain, till the number is complete which he is obliged to give to his master. If any remain, they belong to the diver himself, who may do what he likes with them; he generally sells them to the person who employs him.

The labour of these poor men is very painful. When they remain long under water blood often gushes from their nostrils and ears; sometimes they are struck with apoplexy immediately on coming up. But the danger they dread most is falling into the jaws of the shark. If one of these formidable enemies is known to be near, its presence completely puts a stop to the fishing for the time.

On these coasts, as well as on the coast of California, it is usual for the divers to carry with them a small stick about nine inches in length, pointed with iron at both ends. Armed with this, an experienced diver is often successful in a contest with the shark. He holds the stick by the middle, and when he is attacked by the monster, he seizes the moment when it opens its terrible jaws to plunge the sharp iron point into its mouth.

A native of the country, called Don Pablo Ochon, who was for many years the superintendent of the fishery, and who was himself a practised diver, relates the following adventure, which he says happened to him in one of his submarine excursions. He had been told of a reef, on which it was said that a great number of large oysters might be found, and after a good deal of trouble he succeeded in discovering it. Hoping to pick up some fine specimens of shells, Don Pablo dived to a depth of eleven fathoms. The rock was not more than one hundred and fifty or two hundred yards in circumference.

ANECDOTE OF A PEARL DIVER. 231

He swam round it and examined it without seeing anything to induce him to prolong his stay under water. As there were no oysters to be seen, he was preparing to ascend, and he looked up, as divers generally do, to be sure that no monster is watching them. When Don Pablo raised his eyes

DIVER AND SHARK.

he saw a tintorero (a species of shark) standing sentinel over him, a few yards above his head, which had probably been watching him from the time he plunged into the water. The size of this monster was so great that it was useless to think of defending himself with his pointed stick, for the horrible creature had a mouth that could have swallowed both stick and man at one mouthful. Don Pablo felt ill at ease when he saw his retreat so completely cut off; but in the water there is not much time for reflection; he swam, therefore, as quick as he could towards another point of the rock, hoping thus to deceive the vigilance of his enemy. Imagine his horror when he again saw it hovering over his head, like a falcon watching a little bird. The shark rolled its great fiery eyes, and opened and closed its formidable jaws in such a way that for long after the very remembrance of it made Don Pablo tremble.

The unfortunate diver saw only two alternatives before him—to be drowned or to be eaten. He had been so long under water that he could not keep in his breath any longer, and he was on the point of rising to breathe even at the risk of his life, when he remembered all at once that he had seen some sand on one of the sides of the rock. He swam thither with all imaginable speed, always escorted by his attentive enemy. As soon as he reached the point he intended, he began to raise clouds of sand with his pointed stick, which made the water so dark and muddy that the man and the fish lost sight of each other.

Then profiting by the darkness which he had raised, Don Pablo ascended as speedily as he could in an oblique direction, and reached the surface safe and sound, but completely exhausted.

Happily he came up very near one of the boats, and the boatmen seeing him in such a pitiful state, guessed that he had escaped by some manœuvre from an enemy. They accordingly used the ordinary means to frighten away the monster, and Don Pablo was drawn into the boat in safety, but more

CHAPTER XVII.

EARTHQUAKE IN QUITO.

Volcanoes near Quito—Desolation caused by them—Eruption of Cotopaxi—Story of a Sufferer—His Former Prosperity—A Sudden and Terrible Storm.

THE city of Quito, the capital of the Republic of Ecuador, is situated in the Valley of Quito, one of the finest in the Andes. It is 200 miles long and 30 wide; has a mean elevation above the sea of 10,000 feet, and is bounded by the most magnificent series of volcanic mountains in the new world.

It enjoys perpetual spring, is covered with orchards and fruitful fields, scattered villages and numerous flocks and herds, while the high peaks of the colossal mountains surrounding it are covered with perpetual snow. Highest among these rises the celebrated Chimborazo.

Many of the summits of the Andes near Quito are volcanoes; and smoke and very often flames may be seen issuing from the midst of the snow. Among the most celebrated of these volcanoes are Cayambé, whose majestic summit is exactly on the equator; Cotopaxi, the most formidable of all the

American volcanoes; Pichincha and Antisana, the highest volcanoes in the world. The city of Quito is situated at the base of Pichincha, at a height of 9540 feet above the level of the sea. In such a neighbourhood it is easy to imagine that the inhabitants of the town and country often suffer frightful disasters from the frequent eruptions of the subterranean fire. In 1797 the earth was disturbed and literally upturned, to an extent of 50 leagues in length, and 35 in breadth, and 40,000 persons lost their lives in Quito and the neighbouring towns. At the time of the eruption of 1803, the sudden melting of the snows which covered the sides of Cotopaxi caused terrible desolation. The flames sometimes rises 3000 feet above the top of this volcano, and its roar has been heard at a distance of 150 miles.

A very interesting history of one of the poor sufferers in the terrible earthquakes that often happen in Quito, is told by Mr. Mason, who says that he saw the unfortunate man brought before the magistrates in Mexico, and in his defence the unhappy creature gave a touching account of his sufferings:—

He was a miserably feeble object, scarcely covered by fluttering, many-coloured rags, and his sunken face was almost blackened by heat and excessive exposure to the weather. The accusation against him was twofold,—he had feloniously introduced himself, a foreigner into the country without license, *carta del seguridad;* and having subsisted in a precarious manner on charity during many months, had satisfied his hunger at length unlawfully at the expense of others. I was deeply moved (says Mr. Mason) by his appearance, and still more by the faltering accents and tone of anguish in which the details of his defence were delivered.

"I am a native of Quito," he said (I give his story in a more connected form than his own in relating it), "and would to Heaven I were in my native country at this moment; for I love it dearly, tempestuous and dangerous as it is. Time there passed joyously with me; I was prosperous and independent: I had my one-storey cottage (all the houses there are low, having the whole of their apartments on the ground) and it was well stored with tenants and provisions. Health and friends, family and position, fields, orchards and cattle, all were mine. But I must not allude to them, or my heart will burst!

"The land of my birth—as perhaps you know, Senores—is nearly 10,000 feet above the level of the sea, and is liable to the most awful earthquakes and tornadoes. The hamlet in which I resided had several times suffered from these causes; often had our dwellings been unroofed and partially scattered to the winds, and our fruit-trees torn up by the roots; and even whole woods of trees, huge rocks, and entire houses, had altogether disappeared. It was long, however, since such an occurrence had taken place amongst us; and we lived on without apprehension of coming evils.

"But in one night, without any warning beyond an unusual redness in the sky, the horrible and destroying tempest burst upon us. All that was ever told of the loudest thunder, all that was ever seen of the most vivid lightning, would fail to picture the terrific visitation of that night. The earth shook and groaned, and opened wide beneath us and around us. Forests of gigantic trees were uprooted and tossed high in air, to meet in fearful shocks, and be driven down again upon the ground. Rocks were riven and swallowed up in yawning chasms, or scattered into fragments and dispersed like hail before the tearing wind. Fields of spreading corn were cut to pieces and set on fire by the lightning; while the thunder of the clouds seemed to find an echo in the vibrating earth below. Cattle were lifted from their feet and dashed down precipices, or were hurried off before the blast to perish in the sea far away. Sheds and buildings were scattered about on every side, or crushed by falling rocks, and together with their inmates were ground to dust in the convulsion. Human bodies were hurled into the air, and driven from point to point, until they found a grave fathoms deep below the ground. Blue and yellow flames burst from the edges of sinking rocks; while hot springs of water gushed upwards from sulphureous caverns. Shrieks and howls from dying animals, awful in themselves were drowned in the overwhelming uproar. Rain poured down in torrents, and pillars of steaming vapour seemed to unite both earth and sky. Thick darkness reigned but for a moment, as sheet after sheet of vivid lightning made the horizon visible, and cast a burning distinctness over the whole scene. Oh, what a time it was! Words cannot express what an awful time it was!

"My own house was one of the first destroyed; it was shivered to pieces in an instant, and the whole of its inhabitants were either buried among its ruins, or violently precipitated on the rocks. I was whirled into a yawning cavity, where I long lay insensible; I felt it rock and tremble fearfully when I recovered, but fortunately it closed not—no other member of my family survived. On the morning of the next day, when the earth had ceased to vibrate, and the storm had spent its strength, I feebly rose from my retreat, and searched with a stricken heart among the ruins and bodies around me. Judge of my feelings at discovering no trace of any one who had been dear to me, and that I was the only human being who had been preserved alive!

"Since that period I have been desolate and a wanderer. As an alleviation to my misery I resolved to travel to other countries. I have kept my vow; I have toiled on in difficulty and destitution, even northwards to this place, and there I think my wanderings will soon be ended."

Of the remainder of this poor wayfarer's defence —how he accounted for having eluded the officers at the city gates, and pleaded guilty to the charge of theft while in want, I took no notes; nor how the tears fell in torrents from his cheeks in the course of his narrative, insomuch that the administradores themselves were visibly affected. The scene closed by his committal to the prison of the Accordada; and he would have but little cause— remembering the wretched and uncertain life he had so lately led—to regret the circumstance.

CHAPTER XVIII.

THREE DAYS IN A TREE.

The Extensive Plains Called Llanos—The Plains on Fire—A Voyage on the Orinoco—A Night in a Mango Tree—Imprisoned in the Tree—Unpleasant Visitors—A Jaguar at the Foot of the Tree—A Fearful Conflict—The Fate of the Jaguar—Sufferings in the Tree—Despair—A Gleam of Hope—Deliverance.

THE part of South America which lies on the coast of the Sea of the Antilles which is watered by the great river Orinoco, and whose principal towns are Caracas, Maracaïbo, and Cumana, now bears the name of the Republic of Venezuela. On the coast the country is undulating and hilly, and the scenery is varied; it is very fertile, produces excellent chocolate, indigo, tobacco, cotton, and coffee, bark and sarsaparilla—two valuable medicines—and wood for building, cabinet-making, and dyeing. The population is composed of creoles of Spanish origin, of negroes formerly slaves, of half-bloods, and native Indians.

The most singular characteristic feature of the Republic of Venezuela are the immense plains which lie on both sides of the great river Orinoco, and which are known by the name of *llanos*. Not a hill, not a single tree arrests the eye over all these vast plains, and the only rising grounds are platforms of rocks a few feet in height, on which the herds find refuge during the inundations. The aspect of the country changes with every season of the year. After the rainy season, when the plain is almost entirely under water, the grass springs up green, fresh, and abundant, to a height of seven or ten feet; and when its tall stems are shaken by the breeze, they wave like the billows of the ocean, and seem like a stormy sea of green. In the heat of summer the herbage gets yellow and withered, the springs dry up, and there is no verdure except upon the banks of the rivers, to which the herds resort for coolness and shade.

The heat in summer is overwhelming, and the glare of light fatigues the weary eyes of the traveller, who is often the dupe of the illusions of the mirage; clouds of dust rise from the parched soil, whose poisoned breath sometimes stifles and kills the animals in thousands. At length autumn comes to afford some relief, and it is then necessary to burn the dry herbage in order to obtain a fine, fresh carpet of green turf in the spring. The grass is set on fire in several places at the same time, and it is scarcely possible for any one who has not seen it to imagine the magnificent spectacle of a sea of fire which destroys all on its path, and supplies an abundant feast to the vultures of a number of serpents, frogs, and other small animals which are overtaken and killed by the flames.

The only occupation of the people of the *llanos* is the care of their large herds of cattle. Each great proprietor possesses fifteen, twenty, fifty, or even one hundred leagues of savannas, and from twenty to fifty thousand head of cattle and horses. These animals are descended from the original stock brought into the country by the Spaniards a short time after their conquest of it, and their numbers have immensely increased, notwithstanding frequent epidemics, inundations, and the attacks of wild beasts, by which many are destroyed every year.

The sale of horses and cattle, or rather of tallow and leather (for the flesh is scarcely reckoned as worth anything), is the chief source of income of the thinly-scattered population who inhabit the banks of the Orinoco and its tributaries.

This large and beautiful river is an easy mode of transport for those who wish to travel from one extremity to another of the vast plain through which it flows. But its navigation is not always free from danger, as the following story will show:—

On the 20th of April, says a traveller, we embarked on the Orinoco, an immense sheet of water, *framed* (if we may use the expression) in a succession of landscapes of the most rare and marvellous beauty. It was near the end of the hot season, the waters of the river were very low, and we could perceive, at little distances along the banks, openings through the thick copsewood, which had been made by different kinds of animals as their paths to the river, to quench their thirst or to seek their prey. Along the river's brink on both sides we saw enormous crocodiles lying lazily basking in the sun.

After we had stopped at several places on the river, and had disposed of nearly all our merchandisc,—not without two or three skirmishes with the robbers of these parts,—on the 10th of May, about **the** beginning of the rainy season, we came in sight of a small island, or rather rock of granite, which rose perpendicularly **out of** the waters; and near it we moored our **little** vessel—as **we** thought that there the jaguars **(or** tigers of these countries) could not reach us.

When **our** vessel **was** safely moored, I threw myself into the water and swam to the rocky islet. Having scrambled to the top of it, **I** could reach with my hand some of the lower branches of a magnificent mango tree. I drew down **one of** the largest of these, which dragged **down** along **with it** several **others; and** their elasticity, as they bounded back, lifted **me** suddenly from the rock on which I stood, and carried me up into the midst of the giant tree. "What a delicious night," thought I, "might I pass here, in this fresh green bower, out of the reach of the jaguars!" My resolution **was** soon taken. **I** called **my** "*Zambos*," (half Negroes half Indians.) They brought my hammock, and having fixed it up in the midst of the branches, they left me, promising to return the next day at sun-rise. I was very much fatigued. I soon fell asleep, and nothing disturbed my repose.

When I again opened my eyes, I became conscious of a feeling of extreme pain. I was wet to the skin. There had been a great deal of rain in the night, and the leather of my hammock having stretched, I found myself imprisoned in a kind of **wet** sack. I tried to free myself from my prison, and **contrived** to rise and look round me. A thick fog hid the face of the sun; when I looked down I could not see the ground—neither earth nor sky was visible—water, nothing but water everywhere; no vessel, no Zambos to be seen—the sudden rising of the river had covered the solitary rock, near which our boat had been moored.

I was then a prisoner in my tree; but as it was neither a banana tree nor a bread-fruit tree, it could supply me with nothing to eat, if pressed by hunger, but the leaves and young shoots. A sad prospect for a poor creature whose limbs were stiffened by cold and damp, and who already felt the cravings of a keen appetite—Robinson Crusoe, in his island, was much better off than I was. In order to divert my mind a little from my sad thoughts, I began to explore my new domain. I crept along the thick branches of the tree, which were so numerous and so closely interwoven, as to afford me a solid support. On a sudden, two fiery eyes glittered through the leaves, and I saw before me the animal for which from my childhood I have had the most intense aversion—an enormous lizard of the species called *iguana!* This harmless creature gave me a horrible fright, and I retreated backwards, along the branch on which I was creeping; but to my great annoyance I met with a second iguana, whose radiant tail was describing superb spirals in the air.

Fascinated, if I may call it so, by the sight of these reptiles, I could not take my eyes away from them, and I continued to watch their movements with the most uneasy attention. Imagine the horror of my situation: fever seized me. Seated upon a forked branch of the tree, with my aching head supported by my hands, trembling **in every limb, I** saw the whole country around me under water; the vast extent of the inundation left me but little hope that my friends would discover where I was; heavy rain beat against **my** face; thunder **was** roaring and lightning flashing around **me;** I **was** tormented **by** hunger, and **was** obliged, in order to appease it, **to** chew **a few of** the leaves **of my** tree.

Almost as if they had guessed my despair, the two lizards ventured to approach me. Fancy the effect produced on my disordered imagination by their gigantic size, their fiery, flaming eyeballs, and the varying colours of dark bronze which played over their large bodies. **One of** them was almost **close to me,** when, collecting all my strength and courage, **I** struck him on the head. Both my enemies immediately disappeared **with a** speed which surprised me, and posted themselves on the other side of the tree.

The long day was at length near a close. Clouds of vultures hovered over my head; flocks of herons **and** flamingoes skimmed over the waters, and awoke **the** crocodiles, **who** darting **up** to seize them, fell themselves a prey to the cruel teeth of the jaguars; whole fleets of tortoises raised their broad shells above the surface of the river, whilst bands of monkeys, chattering and screaming in concert, swung from tree to tree, balancing themselves **on** the branches, and seeming to dance **a** grotesque ballet among the waving leaves. In **the** night, huge bats flapped their heavy wings over **me,** whilst thousands of fire-flies, lighting their tiny lamps all around, seemed to change **my tree into** a fairy palace.

MONKEYS CROSSING STREAM.

Thanks to my knife, I succeeded in fixing my hammock securely in its place. I lay down, and grief and weariness, fatigue and heaviness, soon closed my eyes.

Day dawned again, **but** still no vessel, no **boat** was in sight; there was no sound **but the whistling of the wind and the rush of the waters. My fever** fits became more frequent and severe. A mantle of mist, **ever thicker and** thicker, wrapped all around me in a dark **veil, and** hid from my eyes even **the** nearest trees. I felt as if the tomb were swallowing me up alive, I bade adieu to **hope,** and tried to lift my soul in prayer to **God,** as one feeling himself very near eternity. What hope, indeed, was there that my companions could now succeed **in** finding me? How could they discover me among the **thick** leaves and the impenetrable fog?

All at once, a low growl, very near me, pierced through the foggy air and struck upon my ear. I **rose:** too well I knew the cry of the jaguar. I heard a rustling among the leaves, then the breaking of branches, and a sound as if a living creature had fallen from the tree and was struggling in the water. I hoped that the waves had closed over their prey, **or** that the alligators had made an end of it.

By degrees the mist cleared away, a light current of air seemed to rend away the dark veil which had hid every object from my sight. When I cast my eyes on the fatal rock which had led me to the tree in which I was now a prisoner, what a terrible sight was there! The jaguar himself, still wet with his plunge into the water, had contrived to scramble out and escape the death which threatened him. He was sitting on the rock, facing **me!**

The jaguar was sitting on the rock facing me, his eyes were fixed on the tree whose branches fell perpendicularly over his head. He was motionless, silently watching me. There was not a space of six feet between him and the end of the branches,—he seemed to be calculating the force and the length of his spring. Deceived in his first attempt to reach the branches, he darted towards the trunk, in which he fixed his long claws and began slowly to ascend. I felt all the advantage that I gained over him by his position. I cautiously descended, one hand armed with a branch which I had sharpened, and the other with my open knife. I let my enemy advance step by step, plunging his sharp claws into the smooth bark of the tree, his emerald eye still fixed on me with a burning and bloodthirsty eagerness. I leaned my knee for support on the angle formed by the division of the branches, and looked down. Even amid the dangers that threatened me, I could not help admiring the elegance, the strength, and the suppleness of my adversary. I felt his hot breath on my face; his forepaws were almost within reach of my hand. I fixed the point of my knife firmly in the bark of the tree, and raising the sharpened branch which was to serve both for club and spear, I struck him violently on the head. He replied with a hollow growl, but did not lose an inch of ground. He only changed his position a little, and placed his head under a branch which covered and protected it. I saw that it would be useless to continue the same plan of defence, and I plunged the sharp stick into his open mouth, so as to cause him intense pain: it made him draw back a step, but did not throw him down. He gathered up his body like a cat, and put up one of his forepaws so as to level with me, and so have given him a great advantage.

My situation became critical,—his five enormous claws touched my knee, his panting breath told what a vigorous effort he was about to make. I stooped down, with my knife in my hand, and plunged it up to the handle in the creature's eye. He uttered a long cry of anguish and tried to strike at me with his claws, while his blood gushed over my hand. But he had been forced to draw back a little. I struck him again with my sharp stick, which drove him still further down, leaving the deep marks of his claws in the bark of the tree. I had a little recovered confidence and courage. I watched him carefully. Maddened by rage and pain, he forgot the caution peculiar to his race and strove at any cost to reach me: he made a wild spring to a branch within my reach, and received on his head a blow from my club which sent him tumbling into the river. His fate was soon decided. Scarcely was he in the water when several crocodiles, which had stationed themselves under the tree as if watching the issue of our contest, attacked him all at once, and devoured him, to my great satisfaction.

At last I dared to look round me. The heavy fog, like a vast dome, hung suspended over the waste of waters. I was hungry—I was cold—I trembled. My companions the lizards, of which I had once been afraid, but which I now longed to eat, reappeared no more. I chewed some of the leaves of my tree; which, although they did not satisfy my hunger, at least hindered me from feeling its pangs so keenly. I might have descended from the tree to the rock, in order to be more easily seen by my *zambos;* but I dared not do it. My place in the tree was safer; it would have been madness to have exposed myself to the teeth of the beasts of prey below. I saw at once all the horror of my fate. My zambos, thought I, would have returned long ago, if the vessel had not been carried by the flood to a very great distance from my prison. I was nearly in despair. Mournful vultures, with their naked ashy-looking heads, perched themselves near me, and their hoarse cries seemed to foretell my death. I cut off a long straight branch, to one end of which I fastened a piece of white linen. This flag, which I placed at the end of a branch, was seen by no human eye, and soon became quite useless, as a violent shower drenched it, and made it hang down instead of floating in the air.

The third night of my strange imprisonment found me lying in my hammock, suffering alternately from violent hunger, intense thirst, and insupportable sickness: not a light, not even the smallest star, appeared through the fog. How long that night seemed! How slowly its hours dragged themselves away! No sleep soothed me, sharp pains shot through all my stiffened limbs; pain was the only feeling that made me conscious of life. At length, the wind cleared away the fog in a slight degree, and my feeble eye could just distinguish a pale and misty light in the east, the sign of the dawn.

I looked at it without hope, while I listened to the loud rolling of the thunder at a distance. In the intervals between the peals I began to fancy that I

SUCCOUR AT HAND.

heard another sound, like the noise **of fire-arms** echoing on the water. Was it altogether **a fancy?** Was my imagination deceiving me?

Several times I **heard** the same sound **repeated.** Perhaps some **of the** savage tribes on **the** banks of the Orinoco **were carrying** on some of their bloody fights, **but what was that** to me? **They** were not **my** companions—they **would** not free me from my terrible prison. I tried **to rise** and look around, but my trembling limbs refused to support me: exhausted, half-fainting, more dead than alive, if my pulse still beat, my mind seemed gone.

All at once a loud firing aroused **me.** I seemed to awake. I rose, I **tried to scream; but it was a** feeble cry, and none replied. **Soon I heard shots in** other directions near to **me. At the** well-known **sound** all my hopes revived,—the blood seemed to flow back to my heart. Another and another shot, and then I saw a canoe coming in sight round the point of the rocks.—My *zambos* were in it. I could distinguish the man at the helm. I tried once more to scream, but **my** emotion stifled my voice. The boat coasted about **in** all directions,—my faithful companions were seeking me,—from time to time firing a shot to tell me they were there,—**they came** nearer and nearer. I saw them all distinctly, and at length found strength to utter a loud **cry.** The echo of their cheerful voices was soon heard,—they moored the boat at the foot of the tree and landed.

Exhausted with fatigue, I descend, **or** rather **I** fall into the arms of these faithful and compassionate friends, who had spent two days and a **half in** searching for me **on the** trackless waste of

CHAPTER XIX.

GUIANA.

Productions of Guiana—Population—British Guiana—French Guiana—Political Exiles in Guiana—Their Attempt to Escape—They Build a Raft—Their Sufferings—A Second Raft Built—A Perilous Voyage—The Exiles Reach a Dutch Colony, and are Kindly Received.

GUIANA, which lies to the north-east of South America, is principally composed of very fertile plains. The climate is hot and damp, and in the neighbourhood of the swamps, which cover a considerable portion of the country, very unhealthy. The quantity of rain that falls is eight times greater than in Paris. Those who venture out in the middle of the day, run the risk of having a sunstroke, and besides a large straw hat, which is indispensable, it is necessary to use the precaution of wearing a piece of wet cloth upon the head. The prevailing diseases are fever and dysentery, and from time to time, cholera and yellow fever, which make fearful ravages among the inhabitants.

The characteristic vegetation of the country is a variety of beautiful wood used for mosaic work—mahogany, lace wood, rose wood, amaranth wood, satin wood, &c.; and the caoutchouc or India-rubber tree, so useful in the arts. Sugar, cotton, coffee, tapioca, pepper, tobacco, are also much cultivated, and the rocou, the seed of which yield a beautiful red colour; and there **are also** many useful medicinal **plants, besides poisonous** ones **among** which we may mention the **curare, whose effect** is so powerful, that a child **is said to have** died **after** having sucked the breast of **its** mother, which had been struck by an arrow covered with it.

The animal kingdom **is not less** varied than the vegetable—birds of all sizes, **aras, humming birds,** toucans, **&c. &c.,** variegate the **forest with their** magnificent plumage. The lakes and rivers abound with fish, several of which are poisonous; others **are** remarkable for burying **themselves** several **feet** under ground, where they wait for the return of the water to the pools which may have become dry, and others, like the electric eel, a fish five or six feet long, deal out such powerful blows as to paralyze the most expert swimmer. Crocodiles are not uncommon. The forests are inhabited by wild beasts, the **air by** mosquitoes **and** other injurious insects, and the marshes by immense boa constrictors, and a variety of other serpents.

The population is composed of a small number of whites, English, French, and **Dutch,** who share the country between them, and negroes employed in cultivating the land. The latter, a few years ago, were all slaves, but in English and French Guiana, they are now their own masters, and in the Dutch colony, owing **to** the zeal of the Moravian missionaries, they have the prospect of very soon also being free. In the remote forests of the interior, there are a great many fugitive negroes, known by the name of marsons, and various small Indian tribes, very indolent, but quite harmless. British Guiana, the chief towns of which are Georgetown and Essequibo, and Dutch Guiana, whose capital is Surinam or Paramaribo, are important only as regards the cultivation of articles of food. French Guiana, capital Cayenne, is insignificant in this respect, but has become celebrated as a place of banishment. Under the first French Republic, a number of distinguished political men were transported to it, and for some years past, this colony has again become a place of exile for political offenders, who, in spite of the strict surveillance to which they are subjected, continue from time to time to effect their escape. Braving the dangers of both sea and land, the pangs of hunger across the solitudes of the forests, and the teeth of wild beasts or venomous reptiles, the convicts persevere in attempts to escape, which are rarely followed by the desired result.

The following account of the dangers and suffering attending such enterprises has been extracted from the *Nantes Journal:*—

On a late occasion, several of the political exiles imprisoned on Devil's Island set about procuring the means of escape. Cutting down some trees with which they contrived to build a kind of ship, they assembled at length to launch it, but the hopes of the seven exiles who expected by means of this fragile bark to regain their liberty were cruelly disappointed, for the vessel went to pieces before it was fairly afloat, and nothing was left but a few straggling spars. They were not to be discouraged, however, and with the remains of their ship and the root of a tree which had been carried down by the waters of the Amazon, they constructed a raft and placed it on four casks, on which these seven men embarked. After sailing about for four days, they were driven upon a muddy shore, without food, and where there was none to be had. Two of them, Pianauri and Pogenski, one an Italian, the other a Pole, left their companions in the hope of finding some habitation, but never returned. Exhausted with fatigue, they had not sufficient strength to drag themselves out of the mud into which they sank at every step, and it was reported by an Indian that their bodies had been found half buried and eaten by crabs. The other five who remained upon the stranded raft, despairing of seeing their companions return, and knowing how vain it would be to make any attempt to find them, resolved again to set sail, but before doing so, another raft required to be constructed, as the one which had brought them so far was fast in the mud.

For eight days they sailed along the shore, with nothing but salt water to drink, and nothing but raw crabs to eat; but they at last came upon a dwelling where they were kindly received by the inmates.

A fortnight after the date of their escape, the news and result of their perilous voyage reached Devil's Island, and excited in several more of the exiles a desire to follow their example. Setting to work, they constructed in their turn a raft capable of carrying fifteen or eighteen persons. But the love of freedom animated all the prisoners, and plenty of materials were soon found for a second raft to carry twenty more. A quantity of wood had been sent by Government for the purpose of building a house on the island, which the prisoners had no hesitation in making use of to carry out their plans. A square was formed of planks torn from a hut; bunches of maize stalks solidly bound together formed faggots which were placed under the raft, intended to carry twenty of the exiles from Devil's Island.

The day fixed for their departure was the day appointed by Government for sending the weekly supply of provisions for the inhabitants. The provisions arrived at the usual time, and the prisoners, again left to themselves, and in possession of the supplies, embarked without delay. The sea was very tempestuous. But they hoisted their sails, and two rafts, upon which thirty-four men were crowded, sailed for the Gulf of Sina Maria.

The first two days were stormy; on the third, however, the weather improved; but the following night was a dreadful one, and often the convicts dreaded being swallowed up by the waves. Towards morning, the twenty men who were on the larger of the two rafts, came in sight of land. They landed among the Indians belonging to a Dutch colony, who did not give them a very welcome reception, and they therefore determined to leave the place the same afternoon on foot.

Having walked ten or twelve miles, they rested for the night in a wood, where they suffered much from the attacks of mosquitoes and other insects.

The little band set out again about midnight on their weary journey, which being made in the dark and over unknown ground, **very nearly** proved fatal to them. At one time they were afraid of perishing in the **mud like their** companions **Pianauri** and Pogenski; **for they had often great difficulty in** getting over **the** muddy soil of the mangrove woods through which they had **to pass.** Several of them, indeed, were obliged, in order to extricate themselves, **to** leave behind the few possessions they had saved as well as their provisions. Exhausted by fatigue, and suffering from agonising thirst, they **returned** to the raft, but finding that in their absence, **the** sail had **been carried away** by the Indians, **the** prisoners were thankful **to pass the** night **in a de-**serted hut.

On their arrival, **the** Indians conducted them **to** the governor **of** the Dutch colony of Tibron, who gave them a hearty welcome, and kindly placed **a** ship at their disposal, in which they embarked after it had been repaired. **A** messenger from the commander **was** also **sent along** with them, bearing a letter for **the** Indians, in which they were ordered **to** conduct the little band immediately to Paramaribo. They accordingly set sail at ebb tide, **and a** few days afterwards arrived safely at Paramaribo, the capital of Dutch Guiana, situated upon the Surinam.

This town contains 20,000 inhabitants. The exiles were kindly **treated by** the authorities, and taken to meet the other **five** convicts, whose escape from the Devil's Island **had** preceded their own. They were not **a** little surprised to see twenty of their companions arrive **at** once.

The fourteen men who left Devil's Island on the smallest of the rafts, had arrived at Paramaribo afterwards, and they found assembled thirty-nine convicts who had escaped from the penal settlement in Guiana.

The Dutch authorities, however, not being certain whether they were giving an asylum to convicts or political prisoners, thought it their duty as a precautionary measure to put them all in prison. They continued there for a short time, but were soon after liberated.

By a glance at the table of contents our readers will see that, in accordance with our plan, we have given a brief description of every country in South America, with some interesting narrative or adventure attached to each. It is our intention that this volume should soon be followed by a second, describing in the same way the countries of Central and North America till, from the Land of Fire whence we started, we reach the icy regions of the North Pole. In the belief that our "Travel Pictures" in America will prove acceptable to our young friends, we have in preparation a similar "Word Diorama" of other regions of the globe.

www.ingramcontent.com/pod-product-compliance
Lightning Source LLC
Chambersburg PA
CBHW021408230426
43666CB00006B/678